Thank God I Failed

A Lawyer's Suicide Attempt and the Case Against Trying

Orlando Da Silva

entrechat
PRESS · TORONTO

ISBN (paperback). 978-1-0673699-5-8
ISBN (ebook). 978-1-0673699-4-1

Published by Entrechat Press
Toronto, Canada
Cover design by Marie Viala
Edit by Adina Samuels and Alice Sullivan
Proofread and Formatting by Shelly Zevlever

To everyone who was taught that the worst thing they could do with their pain was speak it aloud.
You were wrong. And so was I.

Endorsements

Orlando's book, *Thank God I Failed*, combines a harrowing personal life story of struggle against death by suicide with the intellectual rigour and detachment of a mind trained and experienced in the law and legal ethics. The result is a riveting memoir of survival and a cogent, powerful argument against extending Canada's Medical Assistance in Dying legislation to include people whose sole underlying medical condition is a mental illness. The proposal engages the most contentious ethical and legal issues of our generation. We will be judged by the outcome of the debate. As someone who has recently experienced the loss of a close colleague and dear friend to death by suicide, this book gave me insight into the disturbing logic that leads to such a tragic loss. To understand the true implications for our society and for those who seek to extinguish their pain in this way, this book, authored by one of Canada's leaders of the legal profession, is a "must read."

Thomas G. Conway, LLB, LLD, Partner, Conway Baxter, LLP, Former Treasurer of the Law Society of Ontario

The first time I heard Orlando Da Silva's story was at a conference many years ago, before mental health was something you could discuss at all in the legal profession. When he was done, I noticed something remarkable. Many in the overflowing crowd were openly weeping. Not out of pity but because we all felt a cathartic mixture of relief and resonance with a story of trauma, despair, and triumph in the small victories, of still showing up, not giving up. This incredible book does the same thing for any new reader. It is transformational in the same way, giving us all a glimpse into perseverance in the face of powerful internal struggles and how to find glimmers of hope to keep going. Finally, Orlando uses his voice as someone with lived experience to engage the deeply contested question of MAiD expansion for mental illness in Canada — a debate with life and death consequences that has been insufficiently informed by voices like his. By wading in, he is saving lives. I commend this book to everyone who is thoughtful about mental health among professionals, trauma, and the human condition.

Anita Szigeti, President, Law and Mental Disorder Association (Canada)

Thank God I Failed is a powerful firsthand account of the hammer-forge of childhood trauma, attempted suicide, and its impact on the trajectory of a life, honed through trial into profound depth of character, insight, and empathy in the service of others. It is also a verdict of hope and a surgical indictment of Canada's plans to destroy hope by extending euthanasia to those suffering mental illness alone.

Christopher Lyon, PhD, University of York, UK

Devastating and darkly humorous at the same time, this raw, rigorous, and deeply humane memoir offers what research alone cannot: lived truth. It dismantles the seductive logic of suicide and challenges the lie that we are burdens when we suffer. More than a story of survival, it is a testament to human resilience, to the extraordinary capacity to rebuild, to reclaim purpose, and to rise into leadership after profound despair. This book is not only a memoir. It is a lifeline. It will save lives.

Dr. Katy Kamkar, PhD, C.Psych., Clinical Psychologist, Centre for Addiction and Mental Health

Orlando's memoir is a poignant and unflinchingly honest telling not just of his own powerful story, but also of unspoken and often painful truths of the systems that shape us. From primary school through to the world of law, from being tossed off a balcony as a toddler to trying to take his own life as an adult, he makes us reflect on our own roles as either toddler tossers, or as Mrs. Forresters. His insights highlight how false internalized burden becomes an existential threat, either through our own hands, or those of the state via assisted death; and he reminds us that love and caring is not about abandoning a person by becoming complicit with their mental illness, but about staying with them despite it. Orlando, you did not fail – thank goodness you succeeded at filling in the blank spaces between the false narratives fed you by depression and society, and in sharing your powerful voice for us to hear.

Dr. K. Sonu Gaind, MD, FRCP(C), DFAPA
Board Member, World Federation for Mental Health

At a time when emotionally charged, often secondhand narratives promoting a romanticized medical response to suffering dominate the media landscape, Orlando Da Silva's firsthand account of his struggle with mental illness offers a timely and much-needed counterpoint that reflects the full complexity of human experience.

In this deeply moving memoir, Da Silva reveals how façades of professional success can hide profound vulnerability and sustained battles with mental illness. His evocative book does not ask for pity but insists that hope remains possible even in the darkest corners of treatment-resistant depression. Help, he shows us, arrives in unexpected forms: love and challenge from family and friends, emergency care, an array of therapies, even an involuntary hospitalization that was simultaneously traumatic and lifesaving. Warm words from teachers, colleagues, and strangers often make a difference too.

Da Silva's central argument is as personal as it is urgent: if medical assistance in dying had been available when he was at his lowest, he would not be here to bear witness. His book is a critical reminder that for help to take root, societal structures, legal frameworks, and medical care must create the necessary time and space, rather than replacing suicide prevention with the offer of a lethal alternative. It is a voice the current debate urgently needs.

Professor Trudo Lemmens, Professor and Scholl Chair in Health and Policy, Henry N.R. Jackman Faculty of Law, University of Toronto. He is cross appointed to the Dalla Lana School of Public Health, the Temerty Faculty of Medicine, University of Toronto

I wish I had known of Orlando's battle with depression during our years together at the University of Waterloo; we could have helped each other. Because he has had the courage to tell his story in *Thank God I Failed*, more people will understand what it means to live with severe depression, and those who are suffering will find in these pages the inspiration to seek the help they need.

The 10-point scale alone, Orlando's simple, honest tool for measuring safety, rather than happiness, is worth the price of the book. I have already shared it with people I love.

I thank God that MAiD for mental illness did not exist in 2008.

Nancy Hammer Dale, retired guidance counselor and friend since 1987

I looked at the stars, and considered how awful it would be for a man to turn his face up to them as he froze to death, and see no help or pity in all the glittering multitude.

— Charles Dickens, *Great Expectations*

Author's Note

This is a memoir. The events described are drawn from my own memory, journals, and records. Some names and identifying details have been changed to protect the privacy of individuals who did not choose to be part of this story. Where names have been changed, I have tried to remain faithful to the truth of the person and the relationship. Nothing else has been altered to make the past more comfortable than it was.

Preface

This book began as something I never intended to write.

For most of my adult life, I kept the central fact of my story hidden: that on December 18, 2008, I tried to end my life and that I spent the months that followed in a psychiatric ward, alone, without visitors. I was a senior lawyer. I held significant responsibilities. I was a candidate in the Federal General Election. I was, by every measure the world uses, successful. And I was certain, with false confidence of a depressed mind, that my death would be a kindness to the people I loved most.

I broke that silence in 2014, during my term as President of the Ontario Bar Association, in an interview I had not planned to give and could not take back. The response was not what I expected. Lawyers wrote to me. Judges called. Strangers stopped me in hallways to say, quietly, "Me too." I learned that the thing I had hidden out of shame was the thing that made others feel less alone.

This memoir is the fuller telling of that story, going beyond the interview to the childhood that preceded it, the silence that enabled it, and the slow, stubborn work of learning to stay alive. It is also, necessarily, a book about Canada's debate about whether people like me, whose only underlying condition is a mental illness should be offered medical assistance in dying. That debate is no longer abstract. It is scheduled to become law in Canada.

I wrote this book because policy arguments need bodies. Not bodies in the political sense, providing talking points and case studies, but the real, breathing, inconvenient body of a person who would have met every clinical criterion for "irremediable suffering" and who is alive today only because his suicide attempt failed and a system built to contain risk accidentally gave him time to reconsider what his life was worth.

I am that inconvenient data point.

If this book changes even one mind, about depression, about silence, about what we owe the most vulnerable people in our care, then every uncomfortable page was worth writing.

Orlando Da Silva
Ottawa, 2026

Foreword

This book is not an easy read.

Its title forewarns you of that. It is a story of trauma and suffering, an attempt at suicide, and a serious mental illness. But that is not by any means the whole story of Orlando Da Silva's life. This book is also a story of self-awareness, recovery, and a passionate mission to help others. Yes, this is a memoir, but it is a story of a life in mid-journey. The story is not over.

I met Orlando at a dinner attended by several hundred people in 2014. As the new President of the Ontario Bar Association, he was celebrated as the guest of honor. I was a newly appointed Chief Justice of Ontario. At the end of the dinner, after the usual introductions, Orlando rose and spoke about what became the central message of his presidency: his personal experience with mental illness; how it affected him and those close to him; and what we can do to support our families, friends and colleagues who live with mental illness.

Orlando's message was deeply personal. It was equally powerful and transformative. It resonated with everyone in the room. Here was a leader of the bar, an accomplished litigator, speaking about his own experience with depression and anxiety. The impact of the speech was immediate—when it ended, Orlando was surrounded by audience members thanking him for sharing his story. As I think I realized at the time, and have confirmed through this book, many were saying "me too."

For centuries, even in the current one, mental illness has been kept under wraps, not spoken about in public. People affected by it were unfairly labeled as unpredictable and unreliable. They were stigmatized and marginalized. Because of that, people who experienced mental illness hid their condition to avoid stigma and its consequences. Often to the point of not seeking help in the form of medication, therapy, or other supports. This was particularly so in the legal profession—especially in litigation, Orlando's field—where aggression, toughness, and dogged persistence are prized attributes. Lawyers didn't seek help because they were afraid that doing so would damage their careers. That they wouldn't get good work, advance in the profession or "make partner."

Yet here was Orlando, approaching the pinnacle of his career as a lawyer, telling us about his own experience and demonstrating by his own actions that it was all right to talk about it. That help was available. That the practice of law was not incompatible with mental illness.

Orlando's term as OBA President was completed in 2015, but he has continued to give hundreds of talks about living with depression. He has told those experiencing mental illness they are not alone. He has demonstrated that a lawyer who has a mental illness can lead a full, balanced and successful life in the law. Orlando's advocacy and example have been a catalyst for a revolution in how the legal profession addresses mental illness. He has not only changed lives, he *has* saved lives.

This book also enters an important debate, that will define Canadian law well into the future, as Parliament considers whether to extend medical assistance in dying to people whose sole underlying condition is mental illness. Orlando's story stands as essential testimony, a first-person account of what irremediable suffering can look like from the inside, and what becomes possible when a person is given time, treatment, and security. Whatever one's view in that debate, this voice deserves to be heard.

This book explains how, as someone who has lived with recurring depressive episodes since childhood, Orlando has learned to manage his illness. He describes, among other things, the value of simply being able to sit beside another person, not necessarily engaging in conversation, but just to let them know they are not alone.

This is an important message to those who are concerned about the mental health of a family member, a friend, or a work colleague. Sometimes, just being there, asking "are you okay?" or saying "I'm here for you" in a caring and supportive way, is enough.

I came to this book not only as a former Chief Justice, but as someone for whom this subject is deeply personal. Sixty-five years ago, mental illness arrived without warning in my own family when my mother was diagnosed with bipolar disorder. She lived with it for the rest of her life. None of the many medical professionals who treated her to were able to give us much insight into her illness. Orlando has written the book we needed. I am deeply sorry we did not have it then.

Orlando's message has resonated with the legal community. He has received particular support from members of his former workplace, the Crown Law Office in the Ministry of the Attorney General and from leaders of the bar. Law firms have come to appreciate that providing mental health supports is not just the right thing today, it makes for a healthier and more productive workplace. While we have come a long way in a little more than a decade, there is more work to be done.

Some of that work will be fostered by the Ontario Bar Association's Orlando Da Silva Award, established in 2024 in Orlando's honor, to encourage and recognize initiatives for the improvement of mental wellbeing in the Justice Sector. There could be no more appropriate tribute to the author than to establish this award in his name.

In five decades at the bar and on the bench, I have never encountered a story so powerful and compelling. Thank you, Orlando, for writing this book. We have much to learn from it.

George R. Strathy
Former Chief Justice of Ontario
Toronto, Ontario
March 2026

Prologue

> *I feel hollow inside. I am having a hard time thinking of the future...My life seems joyless now and will always be.*
>
> —Journal entry, June 8, 2009, at 3:15pm, age 41

THE NIGHT I tried to die was quiet and practical.

I was forty. I had lived with major depression since I was nine, through elementary school, high school, law school, Bay Street, the Ministry of the Attorney General of Ontario, the 40th Canadian General Election, and titles that made others think I'd "made it." I fought my depression with every tool available. I tried over 40 anti-depressants, anti-anxiety and anti-insomnia medications, group therapy, and almost every kind of talk therapy. None of it worked, not in the long term, not in the medium term. I even thought "success" could fill the unfillable void. It didn't. As far as I could tell, one day, unwelcome and unannounced, depression entered my life, stood on my throat, and without pity or remorse, never left. It merely varied the pressure. Nothing diminished the core belief it downloaded: that I was then, had always been, and would always be, a burden.

On December 18, 2008, I swallowed 180 sleeping pills and drank two litres of alcohol. Thirty pills would normally kill someone my size, never mind the alcohol. I knew I would likely die, but nothing could bring me to care. In the misguided mercy of my illness, my indifference to death was the single greatest act of love that I could offer those who mattered.

Some have called suicide the ultimate act of selfishness, an impulsive act of cruelty and pain, born of self-pity and self-absorption, left to shatter the lives of those who love you. I saw the opposite: the last remaining altruistic act I could offer my loved ones. I had the agency, competence, and fortitude to remove myself—the whole decrepit, disappointing weight of me—from their lives. And they would be all the better for it.

In the weeks leading to that night, I googled how to write a suicide note, somehow motivated to write a good one, as if it mattered. I even drafted several, but none captured the self-hatred and anguish I silently harbored, without also shaming me into further and greater silence. That night, there would be no note. No ritual. No drama. Just a tired man, sitting alone, in silent decline, deciding that everyone would be better off without the dark cloud that followed him everywhere.

When I swallowed my last handful of pills and emptied my last glass of wine, I had already spent more than four hours doom-scrolling, or whatever its 2008 equivalent might have been. As my vision blurred, tunneled, and disappeared, I fell heavily onto the linoleum floor. My Blackberry rolled from inside my breast pocket and grazed my left cheek, resting gently within reach. Although I could neither see, nor hear, nor barely feel, the impact breached my mind's tyrannical, altruistic logic with a fleeting moment of heart-breaking clarity: I had not said goodbye to my nine-year-old daughter, Candace.

With fumbling hands, I grabbed my phone and willed my fingers to find the letter "k", the only button, randomly chosen, where I had programmed a speed dial. From the trackball in the center, I knew the "k" was two rows down and three letters across. I pressed it. The voice on the other end was understandably annoyed and then calmly reassuring. It was a practiced calm that only comes from years of working as a neonatal intensive care nurse steadying the nerves of frantic parents.

I faintly whispered, "I think I made a mistake."

Although I have nothing but fragmented memories of the immediate aftermath, I know my estranged wife, Adrienne, saved a life I didn't want saved.

I woke up in the emergency ward, sensing no signs of an afterlife.

Nauseous and grainy with awareness, I learned my body had refused to cooperate. When a nurse explained how they kept me alive, I was more annoyed than relieved.

My first clear thought was anger—toward myself. Then disappointment. *You can't even do this right.*

The psychiatrist didn't call what I'd done brave or selfish. She called it a suicide attempt. She didn't congratulate me for surviving. She didn't scold me for trying. She did something far more destabilizing. She took my pain seriously and wanted to know why I wanted to die. Adrienne listened, waiting for her moment.

When the psychiatrist asked questions that I didn't want to answer, Adrienne refused to allow my evasive explanations to land. She simply wouldn't cooperate with the performance, pleading instead for the hospital to admit me. On the strength of Adrienne's insistence, the psychiatrist admitted me to the ward against my will.

At the time, it felt like betrayal. I wanted my freedom. I wanted the right to "solve" the problem of me in whatever way I saw fit. Only much later would I understand what Adrienne had done. In a life where love was so often confused with silence, denial, or violence, she gave me a different definition: love as the refusal to let you disappear, even when you're begging, politely, firmly, and persuasively, to be allowed to die.

I spent six months at Grand River Hospital in Kitchener, but only the first 72 hours were involuntary. The rest of the time I submitted myself to their treatment plan, believing that it was my last best chance to get better.

The hospital stood less than two kilometres from my mother's home at 282 Weber Street West, in Kitchener, but she never visited. None of my family did. Nor did any friends or colleagues. They couldn't visit, because, with two exceptions, I never told anyone I was there.

I was a senior lawyer with a public profile in a profession that worshipped competence and composure, fearlessness and strength. To admit I was in a psychiatric ward after a suicide attempt felt, to me, like social and professional self-destruction. So I chose a different kind of destruction: isolation. Using email as a shield, I told my family that I was too busy to see them on account of work: missing Christmas, New Year's Eve, Valentine's Day, my mother's birthday, and Easter. I gave work a medical note confirming my need for a six-month medical leave; never disclosing the reasons until 2014, six years later. To no one's surprise, my family never called for me at work as if worried about my whereabouts. My brother's step-daughter worked as a nurse in the psychiatric ward that treated me. And so, as always, we knew how to pretend, as a family, to stay quiet, and to preserve the peace. This incident was no different.

My two visitors were Chip, my best friend, and Katherine, a lawyer and former colleague. Neither of them would have known of my hospitalization had the police not informed my first ex-wife, Jelena, Candace's mother, that I had attempted suicide. Upon learning of my attempt, Jelena hired a lawyer who, without warning, scheduled an emergency custody hearing in Windsor, Ontario, four hours west along Highway 401. I attended Court on a day pass granted by the hospital, and after two hours of waiting, and a little more than one hour of argument, the court declined to grant Jelena's motion to limit access to my daughter.

Relieved but exhausted, the hospital ward awaited my return—and so did life.

Days passed in small, controlled increments: meds, meals, groups, vital signs. Doctors prescribed more and different antidepressants. I lay on a narrow bed while electricity passed through my brain to induce micro seizures. I sat in chairs that had seen better days and listened to people with lives very different from mine describe thoughts very similar to mine.

Nothing made the pain vanish. Nothing suddenly taught me to want to live. For long stretches, the only thing that changed was that my old strategies: work harder, perform better, disappear more completely, no longer helped. In their place was something unfamiliar: being alive with no role to play except father.

Tiny shifts began to happen in that sealed-off life. A nurse would ask me, without pity, how I was sleeping, as if my answer mattered. A fellow patient would sit beside me in the dayroom without explanation or apology and say, "It's rough today, isn't it?" A psychiatrist would insist on the stubborn, ordinary fact that my pain, however old and familiar, was not proof of my worthlessness. My mind kept insisting that suicide had been an act of love. The people around me quietly and consistently behaved as if staying was an act of love too.

I had no great epiphany in those six months. No single turning point. What I had was time away from performance, from work, from the eyes I was sure would judge me. Time to notice that the voice in my head that sounded so authoritative might, in fact, be wrong.

When I was a toddler, thrown off a second-floor balcony by my older cousins, for their own amusement, I lay on the ground and learned that survival could be shameful when silence collapsed. I learned that adults might care more about appearances than impact. I learned to get back up, smooth my shirt, and pretend nothing had happened. Even then, no one needed to tell me that my cousins would face no consequences. Keeping the peace meant sucking it up.

The psychiatric ward was the first place in forty years where I was not rewarded for pretending. I walked in convinced my death would be a gift. I walked out with the same illness, the same history, the same capacity for despair. But I also walked out with a question I'd never dared ask: *What if my mind had been lying to me about my worth all along?*

Twelve years later, in March 2021, my country passed a law that removed the requirement in Canada's medical assistance in dying regime (known, as MAiD) that death be reasonably foreseeable before a doctor or nurse practitioner could legally help you die. With this change, MAiD eligibility broadened considerably. The new law included a temporary exclusion for those cases where mental illness was the sole underlying condition. That exclusion was supposed to sunset on March 17, 2023, but implementation was delayed to March 17, 2024, and then to March 17, 2027.

As politicians, academics, and commentators debate whether people, like me, with "treatment-resistant depression" and "irremediable suffering," should have the right to die with medical help, my mind returns to that night in 2008 and that ward in 2009. Had MAiD for mental illness been available in 2008 (or during many other times in my life), my despair, when forcefully self-narrated in the voice of a seasoned trial lawyer, could have persuaded any expert that I was eligible for medical help in dying rather than medical help in living. What I needed then, and will likely need again, especially after March 17, 2027, is protection from my own certainty and ability to persuade.

This book is my attempt to stand as one inconvenient data point in that debate. It is the story of how a child taught to survive by disappearing grew into a man convinced that his death would be a gift. And how, in a fluorescent-lit ward, surrounded by strangers, that conviction began, slowly and stubbornly, to lose its grip.

It is also the story of how speaking the very thing I had hidden for decades—my depression, my attempt, my stay in that hospital—became the most meaningful work of my life.

I'm alive because my suicide attempt failed.

Because a psychiatrist listened.

Because an estranged wife refused to let me go.

Because a system designed to contain risk accidentally gave me time to reconsider what my life was worth.

Thank God I failed.

Chapter 1

The Balcony

> *Give sorrow words. The grief does not speak. Whispers the o're-fraught heart and bids it break.*
>
> — William Shakespeare, *Macbeth*

My first memory is of the sky and the taste of mud.

I was two years old, on the second-floor balcony of our house on Samuel Street, in Kitchener, Ontario, a blue-collar city located about 110 kilometers west of Toronto via Highway 401 and Highway 8. My father and his two sisters rented the house together, a crowded vessel for three families, fourteen people in two bedrooms. My entire world, chaotic and loud, existed within the cramped quarters of that house.

In a tangle of limbs, play, and malice, my cousins lifted me high over the railing and delivered me into the air. There was no time to call out. Just a bright strip of sky and then hardened mud. I hit chest-first. The impact slammed the air out of me; my mouth opened, and nothing rushed in or out. Grit salted my teeth; the smell of cut grass and damp earth filled my mouth as I grasped for breath that would not come. When air finally scraped back in, it burned. Something inside felt wrong. I was too young to name what, as I drew a single ragged inhale, then another, and another. Today, when I hear of broken ribs, I presume to know its pain.

By the time my breathing machine remembered its job, the footsteps had already scattered, returning the balcony to its unsuspecting silence. No curtains moved. No door opened. No adult called. No one gathered. There was no rush to a hospital, only the willful blindness families often deployed in crowded houses to prevent pent up tensions from upending their delicate structure.

Alone in the mud and grass, I rolled to my side and took inventory. Arms answered, knees answered, teeth, what few I had, were all there. My chest hummed like a jar of wasps. I stood and smoothed my shirt. The distance between the door to the second balcony and its railings were imprinted on my mind, but I opted for a simpler rule: stay away from the balcony and far from my cousins. I arranged my face into "ordinary" and felt Samuel Street, real or imagined, exhale.

The body writes rules before the mind finds words. On that day, in the late spring of 1970, I learned that danger could live inside a house and smile as it lifted you over the edge. I learned that the people you love can be the ones who drop you. I learned that if I appeared "calm" and asked for nothing, adults would remain comfortable. Silence, they admonished. Keep the peace, they warned.

I also learned I was not made of glass. Pain tolerance was useful information. And that endurance could mimic strength long enough to survive the evening. Those lessons kept me upright; they also taught me the value of invisibility.

Only later did I understand that unpredictability is its own kind of violence. You don't keep a child safe by convincing him to be quiet. You keep him safe by making the world predictable enough that he can breathe freely, without subordinating him to the mirth and laughter and pain of others. The first ragged breath I drew on the hardened mud and grass became more than survival. It became muscle memory, and then an enduring skill.

Chapter 2

The House on Weber Street

> *My mom sold Weber Street on the 26th for $177,000. She is relieved it is gone and, to my surprise, is not nostalgic about it. For many reasons, I am not either.*
>
> —Journal entry, September 28, 2011, age 43

In the summer of 1970, a few months after falling from the balcony on Samuel Street, my parents bought their first house for $13,000 on 282 Weber Street West in Kitchener, Ontario. It was a modest yellow brick house enclosing nine hundred square feet of living space, three bedrooms, and one working bathroom, for our family of four soon to be five. To a toddler, it felt like a castle. The backyard amazed me. The grass brushed my cheeks when I ran, so high I had to part it with my hands to see the house only a few steps away. For the first time I remember thinking: we had a house of our own.

We left the cramped rental home shared with two other families —eight adults and six children—packed into two bedrooms, breathing the same tense air. In July of that year, my younger brother

Walter was born. Four years later, in 1974, my youngest brother, Victor, was born.

Except for my mother, who was raised in New Glasgow, Nova Scotia, each adult in the previous house on Samuel Street came from two small villages in northern Portugal on the banks of Rio Lima and Rio Vez. They were shaped by a dictatorship that distrusted books, intelligence, and education, and treated mental illness as the source of weakness and shame. In Salazar's Portugal, nearly half the population couldn't read. The only credential that mattered for a man was how long and how well he could endure hard manual labor.

My father left school around the age of eight to work. In his late teens, he escaped alone to Paris to avoid military conscription and the subsequent need to serve opposing Angola' War of Independence. In 1967, he emigrated, again alone, to Canada to join his extended family and a growing Portuguese diaspora from his village community. The lesson he carried into our kitchen was clear and unforgiving: real men worked with their hands, kept their doubts to themselves, and never admitted to being sick in the mind.

In hindsight, after relocating to Weber Street, it seemed strange that the two other families we had lived with, held together by my father's sisters and their parents, would also buy houses so close to ours: one at 268 Weber Street and another around the corner at 76 Wilhem Street. Our new address should have marked our arrival and some safety. Instead, our lives remained so tightly enmeshed that ridicule, scorn, and judgment traveled down the block and around the corner as easily as it moved from room to room at Samuel Street.

Over time, my father's indifferent and austere forbearing hardened into a quiet smoldering spite, fed by whispered questions about whether I was really his son. My paternal grandmother, often in our kitchen, kept a running commentary in Portuguese on my mother's failings. She didn't need to speak English for my mother to understand: the sighs, the gestures, the measuring glances did their work.

In that light, my mother was perpetually deficient, and I was Exhibit A, to her deception. My blue eyes, so unlike either parent's, were read as proof that she had tricked my father into marriage he never wanted in March 1968, one month before I was born. When my cousins threw me over the balcony on Samuel Street, it was easier for the adults to dismiss it as childish play, than to ask what it revealed about the hierarchy, the marriage, or the safety of a young woman and her two-year old son. Looking away was the price of keeping the family story, and its delicate structure, intact.

My father worked as an assembly line welder and later a tube-bender. He considered himself, despite his own father's disdain, to be a multitalented, self-taught, jack-of-all-trades. He often boasted about how he acquired his trade skills by lying to get hired, then learning as much as he could before his incompetence got him fired.

Before too long, and despite his trade skills, the house at 282 Weber Street, and the family within it, began to fail in slow motion. Lack of maintenance paired with indifference, disdain, and disrespect can dissolve the hope imbedded in any structure or relationship. A child doesn't understand whispered recriminations or targeted gossip, as much as what it means to have mice scratching in cupboards and chewing through cereal boxes. Or to watch thick-tailed rats dart across the stove and under the sink.

At Weber Street, my parent's indifference and neglect invited fruit flies to form in a haze over a semi-permanent stack of moldy dishes that filled a sink fitted directly across from the stove. Touching the sink and the stove at the same time would send an electric shock through your body strong enough to knock you to the floor. The house had one small working bathroom, a powder room off the kitchen, where, after long years of neglect, uninsulated pipes burst every winter, leaving a hole in the bathroom floor hollowed out by rotting wood. A soft, dark-rimmed abyss yawned in front of the sink, exhaled mold and decay as its edges crumbled into an expanding void large enough to drop you to the basement if you didn't carefully straddle the chasm while washing your hands.

My father fixed none of these things. Instead, he installed a brick shower with uninsulated pipes that froze and burst every winter along with the rest of the pipes in the bathroom, adding to its perpetual decay. To save on heating, he installed a wood stove that had been discarded by a local family. While the stove burned like a forge in the heart of the kitchen, the room became too hot to bear, but the rest of the house remained too cold to tolerate. The stove burned so hot and so incessantly that my father built a red brick floor-to-ceiling shelter around it to prevent the kitchen walls from catching fire.

In all his DIY misadventures, his most lasting victim was 282 Weber Street. Regular maintenance bored him. Renovations seized his imagination but only for so long as they tested his abilities. The moment he decided he had the skills required to complete his project, he abandoned it, leaving behind a house that was structurally unsound and full of hazards. In striking and inexplicable contrast, the homes of his sisters remained pristine and well-kept. Ours, on the other hand, began to sag and groan as if it was about to collapse on itself knowing that it deserved this inglorious end.

Yet the worst danger housed by Weber Street wasn't the wiring or the rot. It was what people did to each other behind its closed doors. When my parents were together in the same room, the potential for rage and violence hung over the family like a gathering storm. My brothers and I knew when it was time to hide, even before the first scornful sneer was delivered or insult uttered. We spent many hours in our closets huddled together waiting for the storm to pass as we listened to and imagined the terror unfolding one floor beneath us.

My father's rage, though unpredictable, often arrived with dinner. Codfish. Potatoes. Olive oil. Cabbage soup. Two litres of homemade wine. And air thick with tension. For the first ten minutes, things could seem normal. Then, without warning, he'd rise and start smashing dishes on the floor—one after another, as if each plate owed him something. I learned early to always avoid, if I could, the seat to his immediate right. His sucker punches came from that side.

My mother's anger worked differently. Her violence built slowly, then flared until exhaustion. When she was angry enough, she punched me in the face with a closed fist, repeatedly, until her energy ran out. As I grew older and learned to block her blows, the words landed harder than her fists. "The sight of you makes me sick."

Sometimes she threw me out. At six. At ten. At sixteen. I walked the streets until the house cooled down. Then I came home, asked for a bed, and something to eat. If your own mother can't bear the sight of you, I thought, what hope could strangers offer?

My father's violence scared me more. Fueled by wine, he whipped our bare backs and legs with anything close: an extension cord, a stick, a length of wire. After school, my brother Walter and I would sweep the house and yard to hide anything that might be used on us. Victor, the youngest, was never hit.

My mother sometimes tried to protect us. She admitted, decades later, that she'd sometimes beat me before my father could, knowing it would hurt less and save me from something worse. She was both a source of pain and the shield from it. The same mouth that cursed me would, ten minutes later, stand between my father and his fists.

Nine years before he died, my parents separated but continued to live under the same roof at Weber Street. My father built a bedroom in the basement and, for his convenience, wired a doorbell near his bedside table to summon our service. Ignoring the bell was not an option.

One morning, when I was ten, it rang. I was sent to fetch his cigarettes and some groceries for his breakfast. On the way to the convenience store, I crashed my bike in an ill-conceived stunt and felt my left arm crumble as I braced my fall. In swollen agony, I bought cigarettes, bread, butter and eggs and delivered them home, on my bike, to my father who hadn't yet risen from his bed.

Incredulous, unbothered, and without getting up, he demanded proof of my injury by forcing me to lift the loaf of sliced bread with my broken arm. My ear-splitting wail of pain failed to persuade him.

Dismissed from his bedroom, I served him breakfast and made him coffee as quietly as my strength could endure.

Three days later, my whimpering in the night finally woke my mother, whose bedroom was on the second floor next to mine. She took me to the hospital. Concerned for my safety, especially given three days and nights had passed without medical attention, the hospital staff informed my mother that they needed to file a report with Children's Aid. She convinced them not to, saying that even at ten, my pain tolerance was such that she could not tell I was hurt. Even today, she will repeat that story as a source of pride, in me, presumably. I left the hospital with a heavy cast encasing my wrist to the top of my shoulder; the fracture was so severe. Thankfully, no screws or plates were needed.

Once, at dinner, my father punched me in the face because my cutlery clinked too loudly. Another time, in public, because I didn't hold a garbage bag wide enough. The violence wasn't just punishment. It was a performance of sorts. The goal wasn't to correct or to teach, but to humiliate, dominate, and scare.

The worst scenes I can recall (nor ever forget) occurred when Walter and I had to pull my father off our mother as she curled on the floor trying to avoid his kicks to her head, ribs, and back. There is no handbook for separating two people you love when one becomes a storm of unrestrained fury. We simply did what our bodies could.

In these ways, the house had its own weather systems. You could feel the pressure drop in the hallway before a storm. You could hear oncoming thunder in how a dresser drawer closed. Trying to act mature, while accepting responsibility for my own safety, I made rules for myself. I would bring home the best work I could. I would hide the inconvenient marks or injuries, whenever possible. And I would never give anyone a reason to ask, "What did you do to make him so angry?" or "why did your mom throw you out this time?"

My parents loved us. But they were shaped by trauma that confused love with control, and control with violence. The three-family system we had just escaped followed us down the block in a new form. Everyone was managing everyone else's emotions, and no one protecting the children.

Only later did I understand that in unsafe systems, harm is inevitable.

In the years to come, I would also learn that the only thing that made anything measurably better were the moments when someone compassionate, protected by their own authority, but brave nonetheless, stepped into the guarded silence, breached the ramparts, and established a position behind which others could safely reveal the cost unspoken rules imposed upon them.

I lived at 282 Weber Street West from 1970 to 1988. The backyard where the grass once brushed my cheeks became the theater of my fear, and slowly, the forge of something harder. Heat. Force. Quench. Repeat.

That's how iron is made.

And, without intervention, it's also how children become adults.

Chapter 3

The Grammar of Fear

> *I am trying so hard. Please God don't let me fail. Please God, give me strength.*
>
> —Journal entry, January 20, 1980, age 11

SACRED HEART SCHOOL, at 81 Moore Avenue in Kitchener, was a fortress of brick and rules, about a kilometer from Weber Street. It was also the place where the fear I carried from home met a school with its own language. From kindergarten through grade eight, the hallways taught me that violence was a language many children already spoke, and not a private dialect confined to Weber. Grammar lived in the sucker punch in a cloakroom. Vocabulary cracked from a ruler in a teacher's hand.

The school had a reputation as one of the roughest in the Waterloo County Separate School Board. Fights broke out daily in the gravel schoolyard. The shoves, threats, and ambushes were constant background noise.

In the early years, I moved quietly through it. While other boys learned the rules of games and friendship, I studied how to survive. I learned to invent excuses to keep classmates from seeing our house at 282 Weber, including the hole in the bathroom floor, the clutter, the rats, and the shame of it all.

Just after grade one, my parents decided my father's welder's wages weren't enough. My mother arranged to buy and operate Ted's Convenience on the corner of Ahrens and Blucher Street, about ten minutes on foot from our house. She worked long days, from 7 a.m. to 11:30 p.m., six or seven days a week. The income was modest, but enough to prompt my father to quit his job as a welder at Budd Automotive to pursue his talents as a painter and sculptor, skills he had learned in Paris that failed to impress his father or earn any income. We were still a one-income household, hovering around the poverty line, but this time, I had lost my mother to the store.

A gray weight settled over those years and lengthened the walk to school. I didn't have a name for it then. It was just the weather inside me. I did not think of it at the time, but I can see now that the seeds had already been sown for what would grow into my life-long struggle with treatment-resistant depression.

While my mother was absent, I didn't see much of my father either, mostly by choice. By grade three, he was convinced I was useless. I didn't share his skills. I couldn't carve, sculpt, draw, or paint. I hated manual labor. I couldn't tell a wrench from a hammer. Walter, having all the handy skills I lacked, was, as far as I could tell, his favorite son. On the other hand, I was a bundle of unmet expectations or, perhaps, more quiet evidence of no shared DNA.

My plan, he told me, was to learn how to play the violin, so I could busk for change when everything else failed, as it surely would. Yet even my $28 dollar per week violin lessons amounted to an exercise in futility. I earned a place in the Waterloo Catholic School Board elementary school orchestra as a second violinist. My parents and my grandmother attended. After the performance, starved for praise, I anxiously waited for my parents in the foyer. My father and his mother shuffled passed, saying nothing. My mother had to explain later that evening that my father and grandmother were mortified by my posture. She asked how I could not have noticed it myself, sitting there on stage, slouching. I didn't have an answer, and my father never attended another concert.

Once, before grabbing my seat at the dinner table, I tried to pour my own milk. The jug was too heavy. The glass tipped and shattered, and milk spread across the floor. My father stood, rage rising. He didn't hit me. He just asked, with perfect contempt, "Why do you have to do everything like an asshole?" Indeed, I asked myself, "why"?

That year, I was in Sister Eleanor's grade three class. Her long, arthritic fingers weren't meant for prayer but for prodding faces. Her classroom ran on dread, and she used rulers and open hands. She pulled hair and twisted ears. We watched and learned to stay still.

I remember an Indigenous boy named Tommy. She once slammed his face into the blackboard for a wrong answer, while the rest of us sat in quiet complicity. Fights in the yard were one thing, but this was sanctioned cruelty. We learned to read the room, not for a classmate's clenched jaw, but for the twitch of a teacher's hand gripping a yardstick.

Once, a student's finger was broken and permanently disfigured.

The principal warned Sister Eleanor in advance when the superintendent came to observe. On those days, the performance changed. Then it changed back.

I wasn't confident. I was silent and hyper vigilant. I had no friends and wouldn't for years. I was the boy who thought too much and spoke too little, an easy target, and a small mystery.

The violence at school differed from my father's. His came sudden, hot, like a thunderclap in the kitchen. This was cold, institutional, and endorsed. A chalk brush would be thrown to "get your attention." A slap suffered for a forgotten notebook. A line of children, heads down, were absorbing grammar and threat at the same time. In the classroom, being seen could be dangerous.

The proof of my failure came on a piece of cardstock, on my grade three progress report. Sister Eleanor wrote, "Orlando is a quiet boy who thinks but seldom shares questions or answers." She mistook my terror for apathy. But in a room where speaking was a risk, silence was the rational choice.

She added, "He does not show much enthusiasm for any type of exercise nor to be willing to use his time to advantage."

But the line that hurt the most, the one my mother wielded for years, was the verdict. "We're just not getting his best." When she read it, her shame filled the kitchen like heat, like an owner confronted with defective property. The report card was a map of my defenses, mislabeled as laziness. Neglected written work. Bad spelling. All of these were indictments of my insufficiencies.

My mother had already said the sight of me made her sick. Now there was *official confirmation.* The voices from school and home began to merge. Why did this useless son have to do everything like an asshole?

And yet, buried in that same report card, Sister Eleanor also wrote, "Comprehension of what is needed is quite good," as if she was surprised, I understood while refusing to participate. The truth was I understood too much. "Oral reading" meant exposure. My voice barely rose above a whisper in class. She said it was because I wasn't "moving my speech organs." In truth, I was guarding them, the way I guarded everything.

She concluded, "He must practice speaking so as to be understood by the class." But being understood required being seen by her, by my father, and by my mother. And being seen was the necessary precondition to being *hit.*

Many of my classmates were living their own versions of this same story. They endured grief, second languages, and unsafe homes. The official school paperwork only compounded it. We were a working class student body carrying private pain. The system invalidated our experience and handed us the blame.

On Weber Street I learned that perfection was a shield. Sacred Heart taught me that I was a poor shield bearer. The violence of the schoolyard and the abuse in the classroom were different expressions of the same unsafe system, produced by adults who refused to do better.

Outwardly, Sacred Heart was a place to learn. Inside, the real hazard was what people cloaked in authority, hiding in cassocks, were allowed to do to children.

Chapter 4

The Weather Turns

> *This is our sole defense against the season; These are the things we have learned to do. Who live in troubled regions.*
>
> — Adrienne Rich, *Storm Warnings*

THE LAST DAY of grade three, Thursday June 30, 1977, was a final exam in dread. The classroom air was the same thick brew of chalk dust and fear we had breathed for ten months, in a room ruled by Sister Eleanor's arthritic hands. She sat behind her desk, a sentinel before the blackboard—the dark slate that I knew could be an anvil for a child's face. The manila envelopes on her desk stacked like verdicts. This was an era before promotion to the next grade was a given.

When my name cut the silence, I walked to her desk, feeling the eyes of the class on my back. The envelope was heavy with the words I knew were inside, the official transcript of my failure: quiet boy... seldom shares... not getting his best. I fumbled it open with trembling hands; my breath held in the same tight fist my body had learned on the hardened mud of Samuel Street. Then I saw the only words that could grant a pardon: Promoted to Grade Four.

A single, ragged breath scraped back into my lungs. I was granted a stay of execution.

I walked home to a hollow silence at 282 Weber Street. My mother was lost to the long, gray hours of Ted's Convenience. My father was holed up in the elongated garage behind the house, where he worked endlessly on old, dilapidated cars bought with the money my mother earned. A red MGB, a yellow Triumph Spitfire, and other ageing bodies in various stages of undress filled the garage and spilled into the muddy backyard until the neighbors complained we were running a scrap yard. To the people on the street, it was an eyesore. To my father, it was a kingdom.

That summer, and every summer that followed, he ruled it with an intense but calm solemnity I rarely saw in the house. He bonded with my younger brother, Walter, who showed an aptitude for mechanics and other handy work that filled my father with endless pride. Bent over open hoods, lit by a single harsh bulb, they spoke a language of carburetors and torque, seized bolts and stubborn rust.

Their closeness gave me a measure of reprieve from my father's contempt, as his attention found another home. I was grateful for the distance, even as I grieved what it cost Walter. I imagined my brother imprisoned by my father's pride, welded to a future they had chosen. In time, the prophecy fulfilled itself: Walter became a mechanic and remains one today.

My cousins were packing for a road trip to the Maritimes. Between the junked cars in the yard and the vacant kitchen, the world had emptied out. Walter stayed by my father's side in the garage. Victor stayed with my mother at Ted's Convenience. I was left alone. That summer, I learned the geography of solitude, and my sanctuary was a small clearing among the trees along the CN rail spur that served the BF Goodrich plant. I mapped its every detail, including the smell of creosote on the sun-warmed ties, the metallic taste of the air before a rain, and the way the setting sun lit the weeds on fire. It was my refuge, a hiding place beyond the sightlines of the house, and the scrap yard that pretended to be a backyard.

And that summer, my solitude had a purpose. I became obsessed with the steel rails that ran past my clearing. I decided I would learn to walk them, toe-to-toe, for their entire visible length without slipping.

It was a pointless, punishing discipline. The sun burned my shoulders, and I fell more times than I could count, the gravel biting into my palms. But I believed, with the desperate logic of a child, that if I could just master this one visible, difficult thing, I could prove I was not useless. I could impress my cousins.

For eight weeks, I practiced until my balance was absolute, and my feet knew every seam in the steel. When they returned, tanned and loud from the Maritimes, I told them of my new skill. They demanded a demonstration. I walked the rail with perfect, silent focus, from one tie to the next, never wavering. When I finished, I turned, expecting a crack in their disdain. But there was none. They left long before I finished.

It was then that I understood the deeper lesson. As a suspected illegitimate child, nothing I did would ever be enough. My value was a story they had decided upon long before I was born, and no feat of balance could rewrite it.

In that emptiness, I found a fragile peace. The terror of Weber Street subsided so long as I stayed out of sight, and for the first time, I could create my own freedom.

In September, I crossed the threshold into Mrs. Forrester's grade four class, a world away from Sister Eleanor's, though it was just down the hall. She saw me. Not the quiet boy, or the poor shield bearer, but the bruised child underneath. She moved my desk beside hers, a sanctuary that was also a brand of my difference. I burned with shame under the taunts of my classmates, but beneath it flowed a deeper gratitude. It was the first time an adult had made my safety her business.

She gave me a "Happy Book," a small, lined notebook. "Write everything that makes you happy, Orlando," she said. The task felt like being asked to describe a color I'd never seen. I would sit on the back steps of my empty house, the notebook open on my knees, and stare at the blank lines until they blurred. My mind was a fortress organized for survival, not for happiness. What could I possibly write?

"Today, no one hit me."

"Today, the hole in the bathroom floor didn't seem any wider."

"Today, the rats stayed out of sight."

The words wouldn't come. The Happy Book remained a testament to my inability to perform the most ordinary of childhood acts.

Our weekly talks about its barren pages were lessons in a new language. She never scolded me. She just made room for the silence, teaching me that a quiet presence could be different from the quiet violence I knew. Mrs. Forrester did not know whether I was abused at home or not. We never talked about it. I wouldn't have known what abuse was at the time. I only ever imagined that whatever treatment I got in my life was what I deserved. I may have wished I deserved more or better. But I have no memory of having had that thought.

I could not make friends. The skill was foreign to me. While my classmates spoke of birthday parties and family trips, I knew I could invite no one home. I could never let them see the evidence of the cars sinking slowly into the mud behind the house like a fleet going down.

The peace I forged that summer and later in the shelter of Mrs. Forrester's desk was real. I was learning to build a life in the eye of the hurricane. But upcoming weather is always felt first as a pressure drop, a change in the light.

Chapter 5

The Unmarked Grave

> *Tell all the truth but tell it slant.*
>
> — Emily Dickinson

In 1979, when I was eleven years old, my father took me to Portugal, north to the place that gave him life. He was born in Ponte da Barca and grew up in Arcos de Valdevez, in a village cut by a river, in a stone house that held more memories than light. During our first week, he brought me to Oporto and stood me before the grave of my paternal great-grandfather. He had died in his forties while serving as a doctor in Angola. No one said much then. It would be forty years before anyone spoke the truth aloud, that he had died by suicide, although the family described it as an unsolved murder.

Back in Arcos, my father introduced me to his closest boyhood friend, a tall, thin man who had once learned to paint landscapes at his side. I took his hand and tried to show a level of confidence that I never felt under my father's gaze. That was when I saw the pale, roped scars running along the inside of his right wrist. I asked my father what had happened. The question hung between us for two weeks but was never answered.

Soon after that introduction, my father left for Spain. No one explained why he would be gone for so long. I knew enough to understand Spain was close, but whatever he was traveling towards, or away from, felt much farther than the border on any map. I stayed with a grandmother, an aunt, and cousins who bullied me and whispered that my blue eyes and my uselessness proved I wasn't his son at all. They, too, preferred to believe my Nova Scotian mother had trapped him in a marriage he didn't want.

He returned only at the end of our visit, not for me, but to identify his best friend's body. He died by suicide during our three-week stay. The village said little. In that deeply Catholic place, suicide was treated as a mortal offense for which there could be no forgiveness. There was no mass. No eulogy. The procession moved in silence to the cemetery, where my father did the work no one else would do—open the coffin and confirm the identity of his friend. He told me not to watch. I disobeyed and hid behind a tombstone on a higher terrace. From there, I saw men lower the coffin into an unmarked, locked communal chamber, so I was told, where others like him were interred together. No name would mark the spot. It was understood that his name would not be spoken again.

As we walked home through streets that would not speak of what had happened, my father carried a hard, familiar gravity, the same weather I knew from Weber Street when a storm had already chosen its path. I now carried a different kind of knowledge, that a life and a name could be erased not by death, but by the rules that followed it.

The erasure would later remind me of the practice in ancient Rome known in Latin as *Damnatio Memoriae*, meaning condemnation of memory, a process by which the Senate would condemn a deceased emperor to be a tyrant, enemy of the state, or otherwise disgraceful. By virtue of the posthumous condemnation, the state would systematically erase the emperor from public records and communal memory, destroying images, coins, portraits, busts, sculptures, and inscriptions.

This was the fate of Caligula, Nero, Domitian, and, temporarily, Commodus, among others. It also resembled the fate of my father's childhood friend for the mortal sin of suicide.

Chapter 6

The Body Speaks

> *The human body is the best picture of the human soul.*
>
> — Ludwig Wittgenstein, *Philosophical Investigations*

THE WORLD I returned to from Portugal in August 1979 had been remade. The heavy silence my father carried back from the unmarked grave was answered by a new sound from 278 Weber Street: the laughter of new neighbors. It was not the sharp laughter of my cousins' teasing, but a warm, open-throated sound that belonged to Steve, his wife, and their two children. They were a small planet of normality, and my cousins were quickly pulled into their orbit. After a short time, their gravity caught me too.

We went camping, fishing, and cruising in Steve's black Ford Econoline with its bubble windows, a chariot that showed me my own neighborhood could be a place of adventure, not just endurance. Their door was always unlocked. For the first time, I learned a threshold could be an invitation, not a barricade.

In Steve's backyard, I learned to play football. The legs that had carried me away from violence, the arms I held tight to my sides to seem smaller, were suddenly capable of something other than flight or stillness. On the gravel of the schoolyard, I found I could run. Not just away, but towards something. The wind against my face felt different when it wasn't whipped by tears. It felt like a clean force.

For the first time, my body was not a liability to be punished or a secret to be hidden. It was a tool that, in this one specific context, worked. On track-and-field day, when a teacher placed a ribbon in my hand, I stared at it. It was a physical object that contradicted my father's contempt. It was evidence. I held onto it not as a trophy, but as a permit to exist in a space without apology.

Steve was quiet and calm. I never saw his hand rise in anger, only in greetings. His presence was a quiet argument against everything I knew about fathers. When they moved away in the early 1980s, they left a hole in the world I could not patch. That father's kindness became a ghost that haunted me with what might have been.

But the house did not stay empty. The Satan's Choice moved in, later patching over to the Hells Angels, but not before bricking the windows, reinforcing the foundation, and armoring the doors with steel. Mounted cameras held constant vigil. Police maintained constant surveillance. Harley Davidson Fat Boys roared and revved at all hours. The geography of my street became a map of my life: on one side, there was the memory of a short-lived sanctuary; on the other, the unbreachable bunker of sanctioned violence.

My mother gave up Ted's convenience in 1980. My father moved to Toronto for work, and the house on Weber Street exhaled a breath it had been holding in for a decade. He returned on weekends, and the old weather blew in with him.

Every Friday and Saturday night, he would go out dancing without my mother, always wearing his best suits. For the most part, my mother didn't seem to mind or didn't see the point. She told us that she couldn't go in any case because she didn't know how to dance and never owned a dress. After the two self-indulgent weekend outings, my parent's Sunday night transaction where my father left three twenty-dollar bills on the kitchen table to feed and provide for his family for the week, my mother would explode in fury. We knew when to hide in our rooms, in our closets, until the storm of shouts and broken dishes passed. Six years my junior, my brother Victor sobbed uncontrollably while I tried to embrace him in the bedroom we shared.

To supplement the $60 payment, my mother opened our home as a municipal subsidized day care, accepting five children under ten between six in the morning and four-thirty and another five between five in the evening and midnight: no doubt breaking the rules of engagement. Our house, already small and hazardous, became a congested hub of unmet needs for an additional $8,000 per year.

On weekends when he was home, my father kept Walter close, a favorite son chained by his own usefulness. I ached for my brother, but the ache was dulled by a shameful, searing gratitude that it was not me trapped in that workshop. My uselessness liberated me.

In grade six, Mrs. Bernas confirmed my intellectual uselessness with mental math tests. Her weekly oral quizzes were a special kind of terror for a mind built to track emotional variables, not numerical ones. I failed every test. I did not get one question right. Ever. She labelled me "slow," which was an understandable verdict that I accepted.

Then she announced a speech contest. The fear I felt was visceral, a cold wire drawn tight in my chest. We could choose our own topics. My classmates chose hockey, their pets, and their hobbies. I had no hobbies. I had survival. So, I chose the one thing I had been forced to cultivate in the dark. Imagination.

I did not speak about it as a gift. I spoke about it as a tool for human achievement and not as the means of survival. Unknown to my classmates, I learned that imagination's mental machinery lets a boy in a closet build a world where the shouting cannot reach him, the force that lets him picture a door in a solid wall. I did not write this speech. Instead, I wrote about how imagination can liberate a soul and launch human talent to heights far greater than our highest ambitions. I memorized it until the words were part of my nervous system, a shield of pure recall.

When I delivered it, I did not look at thirty faces. I looked at the windows at the back of the class and spoke to the boy I had been in the closet. When I finished, the silence was not the shameful silence of Sister Eleanor's room. It was the silence of a truth being recognized.

They voted for me as the winner.

Mrs. Bernas was stunned. She insisted on a second vote, certain her "slow" student had fluked his way to victory. The result was the same. I would win again two years later in grade eight for a speech about the perils and prevalence of racism.

The track ribbons were evidence that my body had power my father couldn't see. But this was different. This was a nuclear discovery. The very sensitivity that had made me a target—the hypervigilance, the deep well of feeling—could be refined into a force that made people stop and listen and choose me.

I still had no friends. I still could not invite anyone to my house. But the kernel of magnificent hope had been planted. The fortress I had built to keep the world out had a tower, and from it, I had just discovered, I had a voice that could carry. The boy who was taught to disappear had, for ten minutes, made himself utterly seen. And he had not been struck down. He had been chosen.

Chapter 7

The Gifted Lie

> *The mass of men lead lives of quiet desperation.*
>
> — Henry David Thoreau, *Walden*

THE WORLD HAD BEGUN to offer small, contradictory proofs. Track ribbons said my body was not useless. Speech trophies said my voice had power. But the canon of Weber Street held—I was not smart.

In my world, intelligence was a weapon. It lived in my father's cunning, used for humiliation. In my mother's scalpel, it showed itself in the words used to cut me down to size, as she was fond of saying. Intelligence belonged to others. In my hands, it had only ever been something turned against me, often with the goal of making me feel its absence, whenever I dared to believe I could be anything but, in my mother's words, "a snot-nosed kid".

In the spring of 1982, I registered for high school. The form was a flowchart for the rest of our lives: Basic, General, Advanced, Gifted. I knew my place. So, I checked "Basic" and slid the form across the desk to my grade eight teacher, Mrs. Danos.

She looked down, then up. Not with judgment, the predatory

gaze of Sister Eleanor, or the pitying glance of a teacher looking to remove you from the wrong room. But with recognition. It was the same kind of seeing Mrs. Forrester once offered.

"No," she said. One word. Clear. Final. She drew a dark line through my checkmark, then hovered her pen over a new box. With deliberate, unshaking movement, she placed it beside "Gifted."

"You belong here, Orlando."

The Gifted stream at St. Jerome's High School took sixteen students from across Waterloo County. It was reserved for the brilliant, the destined, the kids whose houses were quiet at night.

The checkmark felt like a clerical error with my name on it. How could the same institution label me both slow and gifted within two years?

I took the form home and showed it to no one. A checkmark in the "Gifted" box would have drawn my father's contempt and my mother's suspicion. It would be buried under catalogues and unpaid bills. The silence was mine to keep. I folded the form and hid it in a drawer.

I told myself it was slowness dressed up in a gifted label. My mind wasn't brilliant; it was a bunker. A map room wired for early warning, escape routes, and plausible deniability. It was trained to notice patterns in footsteps and door slams, not in equations or abstract thought. What does such a mind do when asked to relax and learn?

That summer, I returned to the railway clearing. The rails shimmered with heat. I was looking for quiet. But someone was already there. An older boy. Broader-shouldered, with a cigarette burning between his fingers. He turned at the sound of my step in the dry grass. His face was blank, unreadable.

He flicked his hand—just a gesture, not even a threat—and said a single word: "Out."

I obeyed and never returned. The clearing had been my refuge. Now it was gone, erased, as if my presence had never mattered.

On the last warm evening before school started, I walked near the tracks but didn't turn in. The path to the clearing might as well have been fenced with wire. I understood that some places, once surrendered, do not return to you.

When high school began in September 1982, the halls smelled of pencil shavings and the wet wool of the first fall rain. I carried my new timetable like contraband. I realized the fear that followed me now wasn't the old kind. I already knew how to shrink my body, how to take a blow. This was the fear of being believed in.

In the weeks that followed, everything ordinary shimmered with risk. I listened for it in the hallway chatter. In the scrape of chairs. The smell of floor wax. I imagined the other fifteen students as kids whose fathers didn't drink themselves into rages, whose mothers didn't say they made them sick. Kids who didn't flinch at footsteps on stairs. Their houses had bookcases, not barricades. Their minds were libraries. Mine was a perimeter watchtower.

At school, I nodded when the schedule was handed out. At home, I stayed quiet. To speak the change aloud would be to invite attention, and attention had never been my friend.

And yet, there was the pen, striking through my old choice. And her voice, saying, "You belong here." She didn't say, "try." She didn't say, "maybe." It was the certainty that frightened me. Certainty meant I could disappoint more than just myself.

Chapter 8

The Defiance

> *Nothing is at last sacred but the integrity of your own mind.*
>
> — Ralph Waldo Emerson, *Self Reliance*

THE GIFTED PROGRAM was a room waiting for failure from all but those audacious enough to believe they belonged.

My classmates spoke a language of curiosity, while my mind was still a fortress for survival. My father still worked in Toronto. My mother still ran a full-time day care from the house. From six in the morning to midnight, our home was Grand Central Station for other people's children, toddlers in tears, teething, tantruming. There was no quiet. No cleared surface. No sanctuary. No privacy. I was fourteen but had to share a room with my eight-year-old brother Victor while my twelve-year-old brother Walter, perhaps as a mark of status, occupied his own in splendid isolation.

I was a C student in a room full of As. Teachers would pull me aside with the voices of gentle triage nurses.

"Perhaps," they suggested, "the advanced level would be less... stressful."

"This program isn't doing you any favors."

They were offering me a retreat, a return to the failure I already understood. And I agreed with them. But something deeper, something wordless and raw, locked my feet to the floor. A quiet defiance. Not strength exactly, but viscous residue. The same will that had learned to walk rail lines as a child refused to flinch. If I was ever going to escape Weber Street, it would be through this one, narrow, terrifying door.

On the football field, hyper vigilance made me useful. I could read a quarterback's eyes, the tension in a lineman's stance. In 1984, we won the county championship. I was hoisted onto the shoulders of our biggest defensive lineman, not for my plays, but because I was the lightest body available. A trophy of my own insignificance.

But for a moment, above the crowd, I felt a weightless and uncomplicated joy. My parents were there, my mother and father, separated by the length of the stadium. A perfect map of the distance that had always defined us.

I fled Weber Street by attaching myself to my cousins and a group of Portuguese students, smokers, drinkers, and magnificent liars about their romantic conquests. Our common language was the silence of our parents, the hard realities of 1960s immigration. Yet I clearly did not belong. I could not pretend to be interested in the things they cared about or participate in the pursuits that motivated them.

Then, in grade eleven, everything shifted. An American Literature teacher assigned us to read *Self-Reliance* by Ralph Waldo Emerson. The essay was a nineteenth-century sermon on nonconformity. Emerson's message was radical in its simplicity: a life must be steered from within, not by grades, parents, churches, or crowds. "Envy is ignorance; imitation is suicide." Trust yourself, he said, even if the world calls it madness.

I was the boy his essay condemned. I had survived by imitating, memorizing the rules of every room, scanning faces for disapproval. I had learned to avoid being seen by becoming invisible. Emerson wanted me to step out of line, to "trust thyself," but everything I knew, told me the scoreboard was the only truth. Still, if the assignment was to celebrate self-reliance, then my act of self-reliance would be to dismantle it the way a seventeen-year-old might. We were told to make our case, for or against, the precepts of Emerson's essay.

I knew what I wanted to say, but my fear of public speaking meant adding a layer of anxiety that I could not yet overcome. Although I had won two speech contests in elementary school, the demands of a gifted program meant there was no residual confidence from my seemingly ancient achievements. Besides, I memorized those speeches and got physically sick before each one. The Emerson assignment, and every speech I had given and would give for years to come, followed a similar pattern, but with diminishing intensity, revealing a crack in my fear, and the possibility of gaining a stronger voice.

Fifteen of the sixteen gifted students rose to champion the great individualist. I stood at the lectern to speak about the people we need; the people who need us; communities, economies, armies, and countries that are stronger because they are interdependent and emboldened by mutual trust, respect, and values. I spoke of the teachers that motivate; the coaches that inspire; and the unbridled joy of collective achievement against the odds. We were not made to be self-reliant, I argued, we were made for each other: to be mutually supportive; to celebrate each other's victories; to console each other's losses; to look out for each other's children; and to protect the most vulnerable among us. We had to accept that if life had any purpose at all, it was to make living easier for others, and, therefore, meaningful to us. We needed to extend help to the hands that never reach; to support the homes about to fail; and build supports for the families, students, and children being faultlessly absorbed by their own gravity. I argued that Emerson's courage depended on a privilege he never acknowledged; fashioned from a quiet study, rather than an empty kitchen, where the source of his next meal was never doubted.

For students like me, imitation wasn't cowardice. It was strategy. Obedience wasn't weakness. It was survival. I didn't celebrate self-reliance. I issued a restraining order against it.

When I finished, the silence was unfamiliar. Not the silence of Weber Street. It was the silence of recognition. My teacher looked at me in a way no adult had before, like something had shifted.

"I didn't think any of you could argue against Emerson," he said. He called me a demagogue. I didn't know what the word meant and took it as a compliment. Then he stepped closer, touched my arm, and said something that broke open the future.

"You're dangerous."

I carried that word like contraband. Dangerous. Not a threat, a definition. I had spent my life being the target of danger. I had never imagined I could be its source. The universe, as if threatened by this new identity, retaliated.

In September 1985, at the beginning of grade twelve, the football season following our county championship began with great expectations, but during an exhibition game, I delivered a punishing tackle on a player from Bluevale Collegiate Institute that hurt me more than him. That collision cracked a vertebra in the mid to lower lumbar region of my spine and tore the ligaments surrounding it. A single play cut me off from the one world where my body alone had been enough. Lying in the wreckage of that identity, I took inventory. Arms: answered. Legs: answered. The path did not. What remained was my breath and the voice that could be pressed into service if I could overcome my fears. The breath that scraped back into my lungs from Samuel Street. The voice that had won two speech contests, despite intense glossophobia. The defiance that stood up to Emerson. It all coalesced into a terrifying clarity, because of a mishap on the football field.

In the fall of grade twelve, the map room of my mind acquired a new pin. I needed to confront one of my deepest fears. I would become a lawyer. Maybe later, a politician. A man who used his voice and his words as his primary tool. A man who was dangerous to the silence.

I didn't know it then. But I would do both.

The performance ended.

The craft had begun.

Chapter 9

The Campaign

> *Do not go gentle into that good night. Rage, rage against the dying of the light.*
>
> — Dylan Thomas

THE PLAN, in hindsight, was a suicide note written in reverse.

Instead of listing the reasons to die, it detailed the reasons to live, each one more improbable than the last. To become a lawyer, a man who fought with words, I had to conquer two facts: I was a C student, and I was broke. The first required a miracle of the mind; the second, a raid on the system.

My father, who now lived and worked in Toronto, barely appeared in my life and contributed virtually nothing to our family. My mother earned eight thousand dollars a year tending to other people's children in the chaos of Weber Street. The money for my education would have to come from the vaults of the very institutions that had always judged me lacking. Scholarships and bursaries were reserved for the brilliant and the destined. I considered myself neither. But I was stubborn as viscous residue.

My only path was the University of Waterloo's Applied Studies Honours Co-op Program. It was a financial and academic lockpick. I could live at home and earn enough money to pay for school through co-op work terms. One four-month work term would follow one four-month academic term until I graduated. But the lock was formidable. The minimum admission standard was an A average in grade thirteen, a summit I had never even glimpsed, let alone climbed.

Teachers, with pragmatic mercy, suggested I transfer to the advanced stream from the gifted one. The work would be easier, the pressure lower. A gentler path to the same mediocre end. I refused. To leave the gifted program was to admit that Mrs. Danos's pen had been wrong, that the box marked with my name had been a lie. I would rather explode trying to prove I belonged than concede I never did.

So, I began the quiet, desperate work of rebuilding my own mind. I treated my education like a hostile takeover. The fortress I had built for survival was repurposed. Its energy, once used to track the emotional weather of Weber Street, was redirected toward the cold logic of calculus and the iambic pentameter of Shakespeare. I studied on library floors and stairwells, anywhere the ghosts of home couldn't find me. I was reprogramming the terms of my existence.

Then, a door opened: there was a Students Against Drunk Driving (SADD) conference in Gananoqué. For one weekend, I was not the fraud in the gifted class or the ghost from Weber Street. I was just a student among students, welcomed without suspicion. They were arrows, all of them, aimed at futures I could barely imagine. Their certainty, confidence, and ambition were contagions I willingly caught.

I returned and founded a SADD chapter at St. Jerome's in Kitchener. For the first time, I felt worthwhile, not for achievement, but for service. I wrote proposals to transform SADD into a made-in-Canada, student-led initiative: Ontario Students Against Impaired Driving (OSAID). It gave me a podium for the "dangerous" voice my literature teacher had named. Leadership was no longer performance, it was purpose. Then tragedy gave the mission its gravity.

Two months after founding the first chapter of OSAID, our principal, Father Mike Cundari, a priest, teacher, and former football coach known for his kindness, inspirational leadership, and his mantra, "Win with dignity. Lose with pride," was killed by a drunk driver returning from North Bay on All Saints' Day in 1986. His death was the very harm we were trying to prevent; it was the very loss we had organized to avoid. The abstract cause turned personal.

Three weeks later, Ontario's Attorney General, Ian Scott, invited me to speak about OSAID at the Royal York Hotel. In the Grand Salon, I made Father Mike the center of my argument. Before a crowd of eight hundred, I told the truth plainly. The old terror was there, the same cold wire in my chest from Mrs. Bernas's classroom, but this time, I wasn't speaking for a grade or a trophy. I was speaking for a man who had believed in us. The speech found purchase not in performance, but in protection.

The standing ovation was unexpected. Adults shook my hand and told me I had a future in law or politics, unknowingly blessing the secret map I carried. I smiled tightly, scanning for sarcasm. The validation I had longed for from my father was handed to me by strangers.

That speech unlocked a cascade: invitations to twenty high schools, a CBC radio interview, local television. A five-thousand-dollar national award from *Reader's Digest*. When the student activities director grumbled, I accepted the interim principal's permission to allocate the funds as I saw fit. I created OSAID scholarships at three high schools, including St. Jerome's and then walked away.

OSAID grew without me. A quiet army in hundreds of schools. A ghost I am proud to have helped summon.

Gananoqué, and OSAID, gave me the courage to run for student council president. After dozens of off-the-cuff, well-received speeches across classrooms, I delivered one carefully crafted address to the full student body. I had practiced for hours, but it came across as defensive and speechy, with the arrogant countenance my mother considered a birth defect. I lost and became vice-president instead.

For a boy from Weber, it was still a win, a title that felt like both a consolation prize and a monument. I was nineteen.

When I learned I had won VP, I ran home as fast as I could. The first house along the way was 268 Weber. My Wilhelm Street cousins and my grandmother were in the kitchen. Still winded, I blurted out the news, expecting at least a crack in their disdain. Some small sign I had done something that mattered.

I was met with silence. A long, uncomprehending pause. I apologized for interrupting and backed out of the room.

Still, the sum of it all, the A average I had clawed from nothing, the speeches, the leadership, all culminated in the St. Jerome's Student Leader-of-the-Year Award, a prestigious honor typically reserved for the President of Student Council. I accepted it with complicated pride. More importantly, it helped secure thousands of dollars in entrance scholarships and bursaries.

I had scaled one of the walls of Weber Street.

I asked for permission to bring the four-foot trophy home to 282 Weber, as if it were the Stanley Cup. That weekend, my father, who arrived unexpectedly, inspected it on the backyard patio he had built, the kingdom from which he was now exiled, because my parents were divorcing, badly. As he held it, his mask of indifference cracked, just slightly. Something, curiosity, maybe even pride, flickered through. We did not speak of it, or the future. A swarm of mosquitoes interrupted us. It was a fitting end to what might have been a moment of grace at that God-forsaken house.

Neither of us knew then that a large, aggressive tumour was already growing in his lungs. I would not see him again for six months. By January 1988, he had quit work and moved in with his sister and mother on Gage Street in Kitchener. He was dying.

In July 1987, days after presenting my trophy to my father, I started my first summer job at Weston Bakeries on Victoria Street. As a boy, I had loved the smell of fresh bread that drifted through the neighborhood. Inside the plant, that comfort vanished. The air was a violent mix of rotting dough and sickly-sweet cinnamon, supercharged by proofers and heat from massive tunnel ovens.

I was assigned to the Rheon line, where the sweet goods were made. Workers scoffed as they passed my station, known to all as the worst job in the plant. My role was "pan-thumper," an apt and often-mocked name for a job that broke bodies.

Two by three-foot metal pans rolled past on conveyor belts, raw on entry, white-hot on exit. Sugar and syrup welded doughnuts, cakes, and Chelsea buns to the metal. My job was to break that weld. Hour after hour, I slammed the pans against the belt's guardrails until the products loosened just enough to flick onto another line, bound for wrapping, boxing, and delivery.

Aside from a fan regularly claimed by union men, and asbestos-lined mitts fastened with unreliable Velcro, I had little protection from the fifty-to-sixty-degree ambient heat. The syrup and sugar stiffened the mitts like baseballs, making it nearly impossible to grip anything. White-hot pans slipped, branding my arms, chest, neck. Purple welts and blisters rose where they landed. In the language of the plant, the job burned you "from asshole to appetite."

I would never hate a job more. It was the kind of labor that might have made my father proud, had I been able to tell him. Still, the time wasn't wasted.

If I ever needed a reason to study harder, I had only to remember the Rheon line, and the man I replaced, who had stood at that same station for thirty-six years. Law school stopped being an ambition. It became the only door I could see that didn't open back into that oven.

Later that summer, a letter from the University of Waterloo arrived. As I read the words "We are pleased to inform you," for one suspended moment, the verdict of "useless asshole" was overturned. It was the same shocking, weightless joy I had felt when I was lifted on shoulders after the 1984 county football championship.

But Weber Street lived in my head, not just in my address. A letter could not rewrite the sentence I had already learned to pass on myself.

By the time I started university in September 1987, two futures had fixed themselves in my mind: one in the heat of the Rheon line; the other in the silence of law libraries I had never seen. The next few years would determine where I belonged.

Within four months of starting university, my father was bedridden. His breath struggled against the tumor that barricaded his lungs, esophagus, and chest. The four-foot trophy, like all the hard-won evidence of my worth, wilted from his indifference. But I couldn't blame him.

My campaign to escape Weber Street paused as I began a vigil at the bedside of unmet love and expectations.

Chapter 10

The Last Breath

> *Even in our sleep, pain which cannot forget falls drop by drop upon the heart, until, in our own despair, against our will, comes wisdom through the awful grace of God.*
>
> — Aeschylus, *Agamemnon*

In 1988, when my father was fifty-one and lung cancer had begun to outrun every promise of treatment, my mother's friends drove him towards Victoria Hospital in London, Ontario, situated 105 kilometers (sixty-five miles) west of Kitchener. He needed laser surgery to open his airways. It was supposed to be a seventy-five-minute drive, but a February storm and black ice meant they never arrived.

On Highway 401 their car was struck head-on. My father, who sat up front without a seatbelt, as was his habit, suffered severe head trauma, while the others, including my mother, escaped serious injury. On the side of the highway, beside the wreckage, my father tenderly held my mother's hand and quietly uttered something unintelligible as he slipped into a coma from which he would never recover.

My mother, in the middle of an acrimonious divorce from him, would never fully recover from that tender moment. I sometimes imagine it revealing a glimpse of the relationship she wanted but could never have.

After the trauma team did what it could, my father lay in the ICU. The room was lit by the steady, indifferent brightness hospitals keep at all hours. The time had come for a decision. Neurosurgeons could remove a piece of his skull to relieve the mounting pressure in his brain, leaving him in a traumatically impaired condition for whatever months or weeks remained. Or he could be removed from life support. At age nineteen, my forty-two-year-old mother left me to decide. In truth, my father's unforgiving reality dictated the only merciful answer.

He had smoked since he was eight, starting in 1944—three packs a day, a carton every few days—fierce French cigarettes that filled the air the way his fury filled a room. But none of that mattered anymore. The machines and monitors around him clicked and breathed and drew lines across small screens. The air smelled like antiseptic, warm plastic, and isoflurane. I sat beside him and watched his chest rise and fall under a blanket. We were alone together for the longest time since our trip to Portugal in 1979 but could do nothing but wait for death. Neither my mother nor my younger brothers had the stamina to endure the wait, not knowing how long it would be, but I could not let him die alone and would not leave his side.

For seven days, the unit kept its schedule. Nurses checked lines and changed dressings. Family came and went, and then came less often, and then not at all. I read the clock and tried to pray and failed and tried again. I thought about the boy who obeyed the commands from his impatient basement doorbell and about the teenager who pried his parents apart, and about the young boy who moved through rooms measuring distances to the exits. I thought about the balcony and the sound of breath scraping back into a body that had almost given up the argument. I kept my hand on my father's arm because touch was the only thing I could offer him.

On the seventh morning, I was still alone with him. The machines gave their usual metronome of assurance until they didn't. The line stuttered and then flattened, and I watched the body that had filled so much space in my life go still. Reflexively, I waved over to the nurse, as if she could help. Nonplussed, but disguising mild irritation, she reminded me, "That's to be expected."

It was 6:13 a.m. on February 13, 1988, the day the Calgary Winter Olympics opened. Across the country, people would spend the day celebrating strength and endurance. In this room, I would stay long enough to say goodbye to the man I feared and loved and admired and resented and then let him go.

I did not bargain. I did not perform. I stood with the truth that his life was ending, and that love, in this instance, meant not turning away. This was something I could not have done as a child. I chose to be present without pretending. The iron I carried out of Weber Street—heat, force, quench, repeat—had been tempered into something other than hardness. It was steadiness, and the ability to keep breathing when he no longer could.

This did not absolve the past. It did not cancel what was done in kitchens and hallways. It did not lift the shame that had been used as a tool or fix the dinners where plates succumbed to fury. It did not need to. What remained was a clean line between the house that made me, and the life I wanted to build after surviving it.

When people say their parents "fought" an illness, even today, I think about how often my parents fought each other and, in their turn, me, and how little that language explains. My father's last week, lying comatose in a London ICU, taught me something plainer. Sometimes the work is not fighting but witnessing. Sometimes the dignified act is not to fix but to stay and to see what happens. Sometimes the strongest thing you can do for someone who never kept you safe is to keep them company at the end, without lying to either of you about the life that led here.

After he took his last breath, I paused and stood up. Trembling, alone, I leaned over his bed and clutched his head to my chest. I prayed, told him I loved him, and asked him not to be afraid.

Chapter 11

The Means and the Massacre

> *About suffering they were never wrong, the Old Masters: how well they understood its human position; how it takes place while someone else is eating or opening a window or just walking dully along.*
>
> — W.H. Auden, Musée des Beaux-Arts

THE UNIVERSITY OF WATERLOO acceptance letter was a pardon. But only a temporary one. A change of status couldn't evict the ghost of Weber Street. It had taken up residence in my mind, a permanent tenant, paying its rent in self-doubt.

My ambition to trade the heat of the Rheon line for the quiet of a law library was no longer a daydream. It was a blueprint. And I understood, with the same cold certainty I once reserved for my father's footsteps in the hallway, that the margin for error was zero. A single B was a crack in the foundation. A cracked foundation could send me crashing back. So, my first act was surrender. Not to chaos, but to predictability.

I enrolled in Honours Economics. I chose my courses: accounting, statistics, calculus, and critical thinking, subjects where truth was something you could prove, not interpret. I loved the lush, dangerous forests of English literature, but I couldn't afford to get lost in them. A professor's dislike of my metaphor, a bored marker's whim—too dangerous. I needed terrain where one plus one always, and only, equaled two.

I became an archivist of my own life. My dictaphone became a prosthetic memory. I recorded every lecture, every aside, every half-rubbed equation. At night, I transcribed the tapes like scripture with a compulsion, the academic equivalent of sweeping the house and yard before my father got home to hide potential instruments of my own harm.

Waterloo became a map I could redraw, one that didn't center on 282 Weber Street. On it, I built a geography of solitude. The "Sugar Cube" library, with its sterile light, calmed me. The Bombshelter bar, low-ceilinged and loud, became a refuge too. Its chaos was impersonal: clinking glasses, bad music, shouted jokes. It washed over me, not through me. I could chart indifference curves while people danced.

Then the counter-evidence walked in and sat down across from me. For the first time, I made friends. Real ones. Not allies. Not classmates with an agenda. Friends. In the Modern Languages cafeteria, over bad coffee and worse food, people chose my table. We argued about music, politics, exams. The first time I laughed in a group, the sound startled me. I looked around, expecting a slap or a shush. But they were just waiting for the rest of the story.

They hadn't seen the hole in the bathroom floor. They didn't know the smell of my parents' basement, the extension cords, the explosions of rage. They only saw the person I was trying to become, quick with a joke, diligent, almost competent. And in their eyes, sometimes, I glimpsed him too.

Their presence became a quiet, stubborn argument against the central lie I'd brought from Weber Street: that value had to be earned with straight As and silence. They made me wonder, terrifyingly, if maybe it already existed. Even when I couldn't see it at all.

Every four months, co-op work terms uprooted me. Toronto. Calgary. At Mobil Oil, at Coca-Cola, at the Metro Toronto Police Force, I entered worlds that ran on policies and manuals, not moods. Performance reviews replaced slammed doors.

I learned to knot a tie with practiced hands. To a young man from a working-class family, the accruements of professionalism, like the silk around my neck, could feel like a cage, but it kept the beasts out, not in.

With each successful term, my transcript hardened. I made the Dean's List every year. The blueprint was working. But there was still one gatekeeper. One test that claimed to measure not what I had done, but what I was.

The LSAT wasn't just an exam. It was judgment, disguised as logic puzzles. You couldn't cram for it; you could only be exposed. It was, in pure form, the thing I feared most, an authority figure looking me in the eye and deciding whether I was enough.

The University of Toronto Faculty of Law was the summit. That was the citadel. It would be the ultimate, public refutation of "useless asshole," or the most visible balcony from which to fall.

I was scheduled to write the LSAT on Saturday, December 9, 1989. The world was rewriting its own blueprint that month. On November 9, the Berlin Wall fell. People danced on top of a symbol that had divided a generation. Hope felt possible. Fragile. But real.

Then, on December 6, three days before my exam, that hope was assassinated. A man named Marc Lépine walked into the École Polytechnique in Montreal. He separated the women from the men in an engineering classroom and executed fourteen of them. His reason, written in a letter: they were women. Feminists. Invaders in a space he believed was his.

Canada reeled. The air thickened with candlelight vigils and stunned silence. One wall had fallen. Another, infinitely more intimate and more permanent, had been built with blood.

On December 9, 1989, I boarded the light rail train to the exam hall at the University of Calgary, the city that hosted my third work term, at Mobil Oil. The familiar hum of progress now sounded like a funeral dirge. Through the window, buildings slid past like tombstones.

In my mind, a grotesque calculus began. How could I sit for a logic test while fourteen women lay in morgues? How could I claim ambition when theirs had been stolen mid-sentence? What value could my life have if this world could erase theirs so casually?

I sat at my desk. The exam booklet face down. Pencil ready. The room smelled of chalk and winter coats and nervous sweat. The proctor's voice floated above us. What does it mean to chase a future in a world that just revealed this much rage?

The ghosts of Weber Street had always measured me and found me wanting. But now they had company: ghosts with names I didn't yet know, pressing into the edges of my awareness.

I slowed my breathing, the way I had before fights and speeches. I wore the only armor I had left: composure.

"Begin," the proctor said.

I turned the page. The logic puzzles, the neat arguments, the tidy comprehension passages, each one felt obscene, a pristine architecture sitting beside fresh wreckage. I forced myself through them, question by question, betrayal by betrayal. Including the betrayal of my own grief. Betrayal of those women. Betrayal of the part of me that wanted to walk out. But I stayed. I did what I had always done.

I survived the room. When it ended, we shuffled into the brittle afternoon. The sky hadn't changed. But the light felt wrong.

I had just taken what I believed was the most important test of my life. And all I could think was that fourteen women would never take another.

The blueprint I had built, line by careful line, now had a shadow traced over it in gunmetal.

I had spent years building a fortress of achievement to keep the chaos out. That day, I learned: the worst chaos doesn't come from a failing grade. Or a father's rage.

It comes from a world where life can be erased, utterly, and the only thing left behind is a score.

Chapter 12

The Secret Library

> *There is no greater agony than bearing an untold story inside you.*
>
> — Zora Neale Hurston (attributed; likely paraphrased from *Dust Tracks on a Road)*

I RETURNED to the University of Waterloo in early January 1990, the Calgary work term and LSAT behind me, the blueprint for law school remained firmly in mind. My father had been gone for a year and a half, but the memory of our last conversation was a stone in my pocket I kept turning over. I had told no one of my legal ambitions. This was my secret, and I would abide no discouragement. Except, perhaps, from him. I needed to know what he thought before it was too late.

Eighteen months earlier, the man I found was a ghost of the figure who had ruled Weber Street. He lay in a bed at his sister's house, drowning slowly in the fluid of his own lungs. The air smelled of sickness and impending grief. When he asked about my future, the question felt like a final exam. I told him I planned to be a lawyer.

Then I held my breath.

The pause that followed was its own kind of violence. I could hear the ragged struggle of his breathing, the frantic beat of my own heart. I braced for the derision, the contempt, the confirmation of my uselessness. But it never came.

Instead, with a quiet sincerity that dismantled my defenses, he said, "I think you've made a good decision." Then, with effort, he pointed a trembling finger toward the closet.

I opened the door. I expected sweaters, spare blankets, and the mundane clutter of a sickroom. I did not expect a library.

Stacked neatly on the shelves were hundreds of books in five different languages. I stood there, dumbfounded, looking into a universe I never knew existed. My father, the welder, the man who had dragged me to the basement with a doorbell, who had mocked my academic uselessness, was a polyglot intellectual. He had been torn from school in the third grade and sentenced to a life of hard labor by the Salazar regime's contempt for the Portuguese intelligentsia. He had escaped a war, found refuge in Paris, and built a life. And he had hidden this part of himself, the part that read poetry and philosophy in Italian, French, and Portuguese, in closets and garages, where a son too busy avoiding him would never think to look.

He asked me to retrieve one volume: the autobiography of Melvin Belli, the famous American trial lawyer. It was a rare edition, and his last gift to me. Years later, I would find a biography of the preeminent trial lawyer in American history, Clarence Darrow, hidden in the Weber Street garage. It was another dusty clue to the man I never truly knew; and a testament to a lawyer, who, despite his fame, escaped my attention. Yet my father, who had no ambition in law, had taken the time to read about this man's work.

In that moment, at the age of nineteen, the iron of my defiance was tempered with a new, more complicated alloy: grief. I had built my entire escape plan on the conviction that he was wrong about me. Now, I was crushed by the realization that I had been wrong about him. We had been parallel lines, running side by side in the same narrow house, each believing the other was an empty space.

Two years later, at the age of twenty-two, I was armed with the fragile hope that he would have been proud, and I endured the six-week wait for my LSAT results. Every day after 2 p.m., I called my mother.

"Anything for me?"

The answer was always no, until one day; it was yes. Impatient, I confessed my secret. I heard her irritation at my secrecy warring with her curiosity. She opened the envelope. There was a pause, then a readout of numbers. A score.

"Read it again," I said, my voice tight.

I made her confirm the registration number, my name, and my date of birth. I made her read it for the third time.

I had done it. I had achieved the impossible. I scored in the 98th percentile.

A wild, untethered joy broke loose in me. I ran from the phone, needing to tell someone, anyone. I thought of my classmate from French class, who also wanted to be a lawyer, and sprinted to the St. Jerome's College library on the University of Waterloo campus where he worked.

I found him at the desk, a female co-worker at his side. My words tumbled out, breathless and triumphant. I mentioned the score out loud and felt the sudden force of a bad decision.

They did not cheer. They did not smile. They exchanged a glance, a look of knowing, profound indifference, perhaps scorn. It was the same look my cousins had given me on the railway spur, the same silence that had met my election as vice-president. In their eyes, I was not a success. I was a braggart, an insensitive cad celebrating a victory while others struggled. My classmate would never get into law school.

I recoiled; the heat of my excitement flashed into shame. I would regret my lack of situational awareness for years, a regret too awkward and complicated to voice.

But the number was real. With my GPA and that score, I had my pick of law schools. When the acceptance letter from the University of Toronto Faculty of Law arrived on March 1, 1990, I took it. I was one of seven students admitted without an undergraduate degree, accepted on the strength of my LSAT and the GPA I earned over two years at the University of Waterloo. A Bay Street firm paid my first-year tuition with an entrance scholarship. The blueprint worked. The missile had hit its target.

Chapter 13

The Fabric Matters

> *Clothes make the man. Naked people have little or no influence on society.*
>
> — Mark Twain

On my first day standing in line to register at Falconer Hall, the Law School's administrative building, I didn't wear a collared shirt. It never occurred to me. I wore a bright green Coca-Cola tracksuit and carried a matching backpack, free swag from my last co-op summer work term, where I worked as an internal auditor for the soft drink company. Even my mug bore the logo, gifts from bottling plants across the country, accepted before I knew what "conflict of interest" meant. I didn't look like a law student. I looked like someone sent to refill the vending machines.

The difference between my U of T Law classmates and me was in the numbers. I was twenty-two. The average age was twenty-seven. 167 of my 174 classmates already had undergraduate degrees; many had academic gold medals, some had master's degrees, at least one was a medical doctor.

Most of the class seemed to come from Forest Hill, Lawrence Park, and Rosedale. I was from Weber Street. One classmate's father, a bank CEO, earned my mother's annual income in a morning.

That Christmas, I gave her money from my student loans so she could buy gifts for my brothers. We never discussed it.

I tried to make small talk, but my question about a lecture earned a polite, closed-lipped smile. A comment about exam stress went unanswered. Vulnerability didn't open doors here, it closed them. In the Bora Laskin Law Library, study groups formed like murmured conspiracies. Books slid together at shared tables. No one ever asked me to join.

Later, I learned some groups had rules: no member could ask questions in class, lest others benefit from the answers. Helping others was seen as a strategic blunder.

So, I did what I had always done: I stepped back. I fell silent. In lectures, I became my own stenographer, taking pages of notes, hours of solitude. The only place I spoke was in our small Criminal Law group of sixteen, where debate felt freer and judgment didn't hum beneath every word.

In February, the summer job hunt began. I landed three interviews, none with the Bay Street firms. One mid-sized firm invited me to a cocktail reception. The invitation said, "Business Casual." But the phrase meant nothing to me.

I stood in front of my closet, paralyzed. A suit felt too formal. Jeans felt wrong. I chose the best thing I had: a thin red polyester sweater. It was clean. It had no logo. An old girlfriend once said I looked good in red. I had no one to ask and couldn't bring myself to admit I didn't know the dress code. Still, I wasn't worried. Surely the only sins were jeans or a suit, and I was wearing neither.

The reception smelled of damp wool, shrimp rings, and over-applied perfume. Despite the invitation's "business casual," every man wore a suit and tie. Conversations floated past golf handicaps, cottages on Lake Joe, the merits of Yorkville restaurants. Names like

Upper Canada College and Havergal were dropped like everyone should know them. Everyone did.

The red sweater bloomed into testimony. I moved through the crowd, trying to find an opening. I edged toward a circle of laughter and waited for a pause that never came. Finally, one of the partners turned. His eyes moved from my face to the sweater. No frown. No smile.

"Nice sweater," he said. Two words. Almost gentle. But they didn't land like a slap, they sank like a stone. He wasn't complimenting me. He was judging.

I dropped my name tag on the desk and walked into the cold, my coat unbuttoned, sweater burning like a mistake. The belief that my admission was a fluke hardened.

The next morning, in the middle of February 1991, was Offer Day. At 8:00 a.m., the phone rang. One of the smallest downtown firms offered me a summer position. I waited all day for another call. None came. Still, I was relieved.

That summer, I did real work. I drafted memos, sat in client meetings, and watched hearings. I made friends. We played softball. We went for beers. For a few months, the pressure was about the work, not whether I deserved to be there.

It was rare for a first-year student to land a job, but I had done it. Now, I had the money for second year. When final grades came in, my 3.47 GPA on a B curve placed me near the top fifteen percent. I was thriving.

But as I packed to leave campus, I paused in front of Falconer Hall. I had the grades. I had the job. I had the open door. And still, some part of me was certain it would one day close.

The red sweater went to the back of my closet. The lesson didn't.

Chapter 14

The Human Shield

> *The most common form of despair is not being who you are.*
>
> — Soren Kierkegaard

THE SUMMER after the first year had gone better than I ever expected. At a small downtown firm, I wrote research memos, watched motions in court, and sat in on client meetings where real decisions were made. I had done the work, and people seemed satisfied with it. My confidence developed a thin shell.

Inside, nothing had changed. The same thought loop ran on repeat: You still don't belong here. They just haven't figured it out yet.

Public speaking was still the trigger. The signs were always the same: a tight chest, dry throat, and the sense that every eye in the room could see right through me. It bothered me that I could do the written work of a lawyer but still feel like a child when I had to speak. I had chosen a career that demanded a voice, but I spent most of my life in silence.

In the second year, I decided to stop working around the fear and start walking into it. I built myself a kind of training program. I enrolled in trial advocacy, where standing up and performing was the point. I volunteered at Downtown Legal Services, the law school's busiest legal aid clinic. Clients sat across from me, waiting for advice I did not feel qualified to give, and I had to find a way to speak anyway on their behalf in court.

I chose Professor Stanley Schiff's Evidence class, knowing exactly what I was signing up for. He was known for his cold calls and the way he kept asking questions until any guesswork fell away. Before each class, I prepared like it was an exam. During class, my heart raced every time he looked down at the seating chart. *I need this*, I repeated in my head whenever my name was called.

I also joined the *University of Toronto Faculty of Law Review* as an assistant editor. It was unusual to do that in the second year, rather than the first, but I wanted the experience. The work involved reading dense articles and then sitting in a room with other editors to argue about whether they should be published. It was another setting where I could not simply shrink into the background.

In Advanced Criminal Law with Emeritus Dean Martin Friedland, my classmate Sharon Nicklaus and I volunteered to present our class's criminal law reform proposals to a parliamentary subcommittee in Ottawa. We drove there together, rehearsed our parts, and sat at a table with microphones, speaking into the record. Afterward, the late Justice John Sopinka, who had excelled at football, classical violin, and law, invited us to his office and walked us through the Supreme Court of Canada.

I listened carefully as he talked about the building and the work of the Court. Part of my mind absorbed the details. Another part kept thinking, *How did a kid from 282 Weber Street end up here?*

That February, the on-campus recruitment process started again. This time, my marks and my résumé brought more interest. I had fourteen interviews, many at the most prestigious firms in the country. The red sweater stayed in the back of the closet, but I still felt like the person who had worn it.

A small example exposed how shallow my understanding was. Before the interviews, I asked a classmate if I should buy a tie clip. He laughed, not unkindly, but as if I had asked whether I needed a top hat. I laughed along, but I filed the reaction away: there were rules here I still didn't know.

Over two days, I moved from firm to firm, office to office, trying to show that I belonged. I also found new ways to confirm my worst fear.

At one firm, the interview went well enough that they invited me to stay for lunch. I had another interview booked across Bay Street and couldn't risk missing it. I declined. Their interest cooled as I watched. I walked out knowing that opportunity had evaporated.

At another, I tried to connect with litigators by saying that Evidence was my favorite class and that I would feel confident in court because I had taken good notes. The room fell quiet. No one said anything harsh, but the look on their faces told me clearly that this was not the answer they expected. "I suppose that's naive," I added, hearing myself too late. They ended the meeting quickly.

There were seven cocktail parties and three dinners attached to those interviews. I often stayed only long enough to pick up a name tag and shake a few hands. I felt like I was always standing outside the real conversation.

The dinners were the most stressful. More than once, someone handed me the wine list and told me to choose. I stared at words I didn't understand and prices that made me nervous. I guessed. No one corrected me, but I could feel the judgment. One menu was entirely in Italian, one continuous list with no headings. When they asked me to order first, I had no idea which items were appetizers, and which were the main courses. Even though I was only twenty-two, I was too embarrassed to ask. I chose one from near the top, one from the middle, and one from the bottom. The meal that followed —three different antipasto plates—made it obvious I didn't know what I was doing. That was the last time I heard from that firm.

On the second morning, I was exhausted. At my first interview of the day, they asked about my undergraduate thesis. My mind went blank. I couldn't remember the topic. The student escort stepped out to make a call and then walked me straight to the elevators. I knew what that meant.

But one dinner was different.

The lawyers at that table seemed more relaxed. They didn't ask about golf, boats, or country clubs. One of them told a story about renting a cottage and discovering dozens of chicken wishbones stuck to the walls, just below the ceiling, in every room.

Without planning it, I heard myself say, "Was it advertised as the Salmonella Surprise?"

They genuinely laughed.

The next morning, they called me. McMillan Binch, which had once been the law firm of Prime Minister John Turner, offered me a summer job. I accepted. A year later, they offered me an articling position. The one genuine connection I made during a recruiting dinner at a fancy restaurant landed me a job—two, in fact.

For years, my dream had been to practice criminal law. That was the picture in my head from grade eleven onward: standing in court, speaking for people who had no one in their corner. But at University of Toronto's law program in the early 1990s, there was a clear ranking. The students who were seen as successful did not aim to become legal aid or duty counsel. They set their sights for Bay Street or Wall Street to launch their careers in corporate-commercial work, securities, and mergers and acquisitions while heading, without rest, toward the ultimate presumptive marker of success, partnership at prestigious law firm. In allowing others to define success for me, I reframed my dream and abandoned criminal law.

I told myself corporate-commercial litigation was the better path. Accepting the offer from McMillan Binch felt like proof that I was doing what you were supposed to do if you were serious.

By the end of third year, I was invited to be Co-Editor-in-Chief of the *University of Toronto Faculty of Law Review*, along with someone who would become a close friend. I now had the firm, the grades, the journal, and the title.

From the outside, it looked like a straight, upward climb. The boy from Weber Street had made it to the top of one of the most competitive law schools in the country and secured a place at a major firm.

From the inside, something else was taking shape. Each new achievement gave me a brief sense of safety and then joined the others as further proof that I could not afford to fail. I was not building a life so much as building a shield—layer after layer of roles, honors, and positions between the world and the part of me that still believed I was worthless.

Chapter 15

The Stone Face

> *The stone face seemed to have stuck. It stayed with him all the time, when he was in school, even at night when he woke up and listened to the old house creak and groan.*
>
> — Paula Cox, *The Stone-faced Boy* (1968)

My third year should have been a victory lap. *The Law Review*, the articling offer, the respect, it was all there, laid out like a Vegas buffet. But I had no appetite.

The voice in my head, the one that sounded like mine but used Weber Street's logic, had the last word. It looked at everything I'd worked for and called it nothing.

What settled over me wasn't new. It was a familiar weather system returning. Not sudden panic, but the same low pressure that used to fill the house before my father opened the door. Depression wasn't a formal diagnosis. It lived within me as a growing sense of self worthlessness, the ugly personification of the useless asshole, the person without friends, without hope, numb to any pleasure, convinced it would never improve and never should simply because I deserved nothing better. My depression was Weber Street reconstructed within my skull, dictating my worth using its most persuasive and compelling voice: my own.

I trained my face to stay neutral, stone-faced, in fact. I kept my voice steady. I offered the world a narrow range of expressions: focused, too busy, and always "fine." It was the same skill I'd used as a boy, smoothing my shirt on the hardened mud under the balcony, and walking into the house as if nothing happened. Back then, I performed "normal" to relax the room. Now, I performed "competent" to evade the notice of a judgmental profession.

Inside, my mind turned on itself. The conclusion was simple and relentless: my achievements were not a cure. Nothing was. More success could never change how I felt.

I had already tested what happened when you unmask need. In first year, after I admitted to a classmate that I was struggling, she said, "You're just fishing for compliments." The lesson was clear: need was unattractive at best, manipulative at worst. In law school and in court, a lawyer is hired to be steady and strong. No one wants to see the cracks.

That fall, my withdrawal became complete. A six-year relationship ended, in part because I had already left it. I had gone somewhere inside myself that she couldn't reach. A four-month rebound relationship followed the same pattern. She saw the strain, said she couldn't carry it, and walked away. With them went the last people who knew me well enough to ask what was wrong.

From about the age of eight, my mother had a nickname for me. "Chief Dark Cloud," she'd say, after a cartoon character who walked under his own rainstorm. She laughed when she said it. I didn't. The barb hit its mark and settled in. No matter the weather, I brought the rain.

Other women supplied the rest of the verdict:

"Your need for reassurance is a turnoff."

"Are you a man, or not?"

"If you're depressed, it's because you want to be."

The content varied; the message did not. There was no obvious reason for my sadness. The problem was not the past, the pressure, or the work. The problem was me. Something basic was wrong. I was defective.

So, I hid the flaw and doubled down on the only cure I still believed: making partner. That title at a major firm would silence the voice in my head. It would show everyone, including me, that I was not useless, not weak, not broken, but possibly still an asshole, and deeply rewarded for being one. If I failed, I would confirm everything Weber Street had ever said about me and which, despite everything, I still believed.

I graduated. My cumulative GPA was 3.33. I helped lead the *Law Review*. By every meaningful standard, I was ready.

In May 1993, I stood at the next gate. McMillan Binch hired twenty-five articling students. They would keep six or seven. I was desperate to be one of them.

Chapter 16

The Glass

> *The strongest man in the world is he who stands most alone.*
>
> — Henrik Ibsen, *An Enemy of the People*

FOR THE PERFORMANCE OF COMPETENCE, I needed a role model before I set foot inside McMillan Binch to start my articling year in July 1993. That spring I found one. His name was Nigel Wright. Although he was only five years my senior, he had already made partner at Davies, Ward, and Beck, a prestigious Bay Street law firm, and was, at that time, also serving as an adjunct professor at the University of Toronto Faculty of Law, teaching negotiation. To me, he seemed to possess every attribute a successful lawyer needed while unintentionally, but importantly, revealing each one I lacked. I did what I could to emulate him long after we lost contact, starting with a brief foray into politics in the spring of 1993.

A former speechwriter and brilliant young lawyer, Nigel was the head of policy for Kim Campbell's campaign to become Canada's next prime minister. My presence on the campaign team was not significant enough to warrant a title, but my real role was to learn how to pursue "success" with flawless execution despite not knowing what the word meant for me. I simply wanted what others thought amounted to success. And for a few weeks that spring, I was surrounded by it.

Nigel, at thirty years old, was a marvel of human engineering. He worked from 5:00 a.m. until 1:00 a.m., and most days had already run a half-marathon before others had coffee. He was the first to arrive and the last to leave, a study in tireless discipline. He was generous with his time, humble in manner. And his armor was perfect. No cracks. Ever.

Nigel didn't have edges; he had surfaces. Smooth. Composed. Impossibly consistent. Always calm. Intelligent beyond measure. But I never knew if he was happy. I never knew if the man who had perfected the stone face ever felt the strain of holding it in place.

He showed me the summit of the mountain I set myself to climb, and the sight of it filled me with dread more than inspiration. I feared I'd never have the strength to reach what seemed necessary to justify the space I occupied. Or worse yet, that I would reach it and discover a want of meaning—a hollow victory at enormous cost.

On June 13, 1993, Kim Campbell won the leadership of the Progressive Conservative Party at its leadership convention in Ottawa against Jean Charest. Campbell beat Charest on the second ballot by 187 votes. I was twenty-five at the time and was only allowed to attend the convention because of media credentials kindly provided by the *Peace River Record Gazette* in exchange for an article describing the experience. That experience, just being there and breathing in its energy, was important to me, because my father, now gone for five years, had been a big fan of political theater.

We rarely watched television together, but between 1976 and 1980, we never seemed to miss a political convention or referendum speech on one of the three television channels we received. Usually,

Walter and I had to take turns holding the rabbit ear antenna to maintain reception. To have had the chance to attend a real political convention in person, on account of having attended law school and earning the confidence of Nigel Wright, was something, I imagine, would have pleased my father.

Five days after the convention, on June 18, 1993, I attended Convocation Hall at the University of Toronto to receive my law degree. The last time I was there, in 1991, the Law School marked the opening of its new Bora Laskin Law Library, named after the late great Chief Justice of Canada, who had been appointed by Prime Minister Pierre Trudeau, my father's hero. The former Prime Minister addressed the audience, referred to Prime Minister Mulroney as a "sorcerer's apprentice", and bowed his head to receive his Honorary Doctor of Laws.

Five days after I received my law degree at Convocation Hall, Kim Campbell was sworn in as Canada's nineteenth and first woman Prime Minister of Canada. Her tenure amounted to a "summer job", in the infamous words of her successor, Prime Minister Jean Chretien, whose Liberal Party of Canada won the General Election so decisively that the PC Party was reduced to only two seats in the House of Commons. Campbell's seat was not among them.

After the spring of 1993, I would never see Nigel Wright again, though many years later we resumed irregular contact on LinkedIn. He returned to Davies, and then moved to Onex, and then eventually served as the Chief of Staff to Prime Minister Stephen Harper, before returning to serve as Managing Partner at Onex's office in London, England. During the evening of September 30, 2025, the heart that carried Nigel though daily half marathons before dawn since at least the early 1990s stopped beating, ending a remarkable life tragically soon. Nigel was sixty-two.

I committed to try, during my articling year and beyond, to emulate, with fractional success, Nigel's work ethic, discipline, intelligence, and persistence. The endless drumbeat pacing my effort—

work harder, stay later, show nothing—while my mind's bugle sounded each failure.

I started articling at McMillan Binch on Monday, July 5, 1993. For four days, I learned the rituals of floors thirty-five to thirty-eight, including the hum of the printers, the weight of the bond paper, and the precise hierarchy of a law firm's kitchen.

On Friday, July 9, 1993, a popular, hardworking, and kind lawyer named Garry Hoy, thirty-nine, died. He was a partner at another firm, Holden Day Wilson. While giving a tour to articling students, including some from my Law School class, he tried to entertain them using one of his party tricks. To prove the engineered strength of the tower's windows, Garry threw himself against the glass expecting it to bounce him back into the room as it always had before. Instead, the frame gave way, and Garry fell twenty-four storeys onto a concrete bench in the courtyard surrounded by the office complex known as the Toronto-Dominion Centre, one of the most prestigious business addresses in Canada.

The news reached my floor in shocked whispers. One of my new colleagues claimed to have witnessed the immediate aftermath, sparing us no details. People said the firm would never recover. By 1996, Holden Day Wilson, a pillar of Toronto's Bay Street culture, unravelled in what was, at that time, the largest law firm closure in Canada. A recent merger and Garry's death produced too much load for its walls to bear.

The following Monday morning, July 12, 1993, a Royal Bank Plaza memo warned us not to throw our bodies against the windows. The firm followed it with a second memo reminding us not to use the ice cubes. They were for clients only.

For my part, having lived the most eventful summer of my life, I looked out at the thirty-seventh-floor window of my new golden tower and imagined Garry's final thoughts as the frame gave way.

The city stretched below, hard and glittering. I asked myself whether I was a Nigel or a Garry, when really, I seemed I could be neither; though both were held up as standards for the success I chased to fill the void Weber Street carved out of me.

I had spent a lifetime building my own pane of glass, a surface of competence and calm. I pressed my hand against the cool, unbroken window in front of me. And for the first time, I wondered about the frame.

Chapter 17

The Golden Tower

> *Ah, but a man's reach should exceed his grasp, Or what's heaven for?*
>
> — Robert Browning, *Andrea del Sarto*

THE ROYAL BANK PLAZA, the golden tower at the bottom of Bay Street in Toronto, had its golden rules: window offices were not for students, ice cubes were for clients, and students could not refuse work.

Twenty-five of us entered its mirrored membrane in July of 1993, the city still in the long shudder of recession. We were its unlikely beneficiaries, cheap, intelligent labor, hired in a batch of twenty-five with the understanding that six, maybe seven, would be asked to stay on as an associate lawyer. These were the students that would be "hired back." The rest would have to find another path to success. The math was never stated, only absorbed through the pores: we were a controlled burn, and most of us were the fuel.

At McMillan Binch, our student officers were windowless, as was the library, and all kitchens and lounges. We were paired in rooms the color of old Xerox machines, under fluorescent tubes that hummed a constant B-flat of institutional fatigue. We billed at $90 an hour, a figure that felt less like value and more like a taunt. The light we worked under long into the night was borrowed from the hallway; the air, recirculated from some deeper, unseen lung of the building. We were not apprentices in a guild. We were processors in a clean, quiet machine.

The kitchen lesson came in the first week. "Those are for clients," a law clerk said, referring to the ice. Her voice wasn't unkind. It was factual, like a tour guide noting a historical boundary, but it reminded us of the unspoken curriculum we were all studying: the hierarchy of printers (the fastest were reserved for the work of partners on the floor), the sacred silence of the thirty-seventh-floor library after 8 p.m., the way a partner's open door was a display case, not an invitation.

If the tower was the frame, 40 Gerrard Street East was the life wedged inside it. The walk home was my decompression. The chill of climate control gave way to the humid wall of a Toronto summer, then to the damp cellar smell of my building's stairwell. The apartment cost $750 a month on a $37,000 salary, about what my father had earned as a tube-bender on the assembly line at McDonnell Douglas in Mississauga the year he died, three times my mother's income. To the unaware, it might have looked like success. In practice, it was a sparsely furnished one bedroom enclosure with a frameless futon on gray carpet and formless hope on credit.

For the first three weeks, I slept on the floor of what was my first solo apartment in downtown Toronto. Before my first pay, my bed was a Samsonite suit bag stuffed with dirty laundry, a nest that smelled of dry-cleaner chemicals and sweat. The fridge contained exactly one item: a half-box of Cow Brand baking soda left by the previous tenant. Sometimes I'd open the door just to see its stark white carton in the empty light, and to take in the irony of my unnecessary austerity. If I could ever relieve the ruminating depressive compression in my head, I really didn't need much. I never had, nor much desired, nice things.

The cockroaches were my true overlords. They were fast, but too slow to escape my disgust. Flick on the kitchen light and half a dozen would scatter with a sound like crinkling cellophane. I'd find them in the cutlery drawer, behind the toilet, once in my shoe. At night, lying on the floor, I'd feel the phantom itch of them crawling over me, a grim acknowledgement of shared tenancy.

The plumbing announced itself violently. The first time I turned the shower dial, the diverter valve exploded. A chunk of ceramic shot out, followed by a spray of water and wet plaster. I stood there, holding the shower head like a useless weapon. For two weeks I bathed across the street at the Toronto Metropolitan University (then, Ryerson University) athletic center, a ghost among undergraduates, scrubbing away the previous day's fatigue under institutional shower heads in one large room.

My only furniture arrived courtesy of my high school friend, Chip: a gold fabric recliner, formerly his grandmother's. "It's got some miles on it," he said, grinning. He'd tried to clean it, but it retained a faint, persistent odor of urine. We placed it in the center of the empty living room. Later I bought a $125 futon and laid it directly on the floor. My kingdom: a urine-scented throne and a thin mattress on gray carpet.

None of it truly fazed me. This was not Weber Street squalor. This was almost monastic. The cockroaches were insects, not omens. The empty fridge was monument to time spent endlessly working. The exploding shower was a mechanical failure that tracked with my childhood experience. Still, the apartment, like the railway clearing had once been, was a reprieve from others, in this case, those who watched, judged, or billed time.

The real pressure was in the tower. That was where the rules of your self-worth were written. The work lived in three places: our cramped offices, the windowless library, and the photocopy-and-binding room.

The library's silence was the worst kind, not peaceful, but thick with absorbed panic. It was the silence of young minds screaming quietly at statutes. The carpet, gray and deep, swallowed the sound. I spent hours there, often next to a guy named David from UBC, who clicked his pen exactly three times before going back to the Canadian Abridgment. We never really connected. Our camaraderie was the shared rhythm of turning pages and reaching, in tandem, for the next volume.

The rules weren't just in the case law; they were taped to walls, like the memo reminding us that ice cubes were for clients. It was a tiny thing, but it made the hierarchy unmistakable: partners and clients first, students somewhere below the level of frozen water.

The photocopy-and-binding room was different from the library: hot, loud, and purely mechanical. The abstract terror of the law gave way to simple physics with rhythmic pulses of light, rubber belts driving paper through rolling gears, and the heavy smell of black toner. My first late-night solo copy and binding job was for a multi-million-dollar transaction closing at midnight. I stood over the Cerlox binding machine, feeding pages and throwing my weight into the handle while the copier whirled and jammed with chaotic fury. Whenever it seized, I pried the crumpled document out with a letter opener, my fingers burnt and black with ink, silently begging the godforsaken machine to start again. In that moment, I wasn't afraid of failing at law. I was afraid of ruining the paper.

The work itself methodically and competently transformed a client's uncertainty and risk into billable predictability, measured in six-minute intervals; often, but not always, achieving best possible outcomes for partners and clients alike.

My first real assignment came from a partner named Carson. He popped his head into my office at 4:55 p.m. on a Tuesday, tossed a green litigation folder onto my desk, and said, "The limitation period argument in the Kruk case. There's a line of cases from Newfoundland that might save us. Find them. Memo by nine tomorrow."

The Kruk file arrived in four brown accordion files, each four inches thick and fourteen inches long. They contained color-coded subfolders organizing documents labeled "pleadings," "correspondence," "research," "privileged," and "productions." Each lawyer had their own system. I didn't know what created the limitation period or how to overcome it with legal arguments. I didn't even know what Kruk was about. Newfoundland jurisprudence was a blank continent in my mind, but law school taught me how to research, analyze, and write.

I started in the library. By midnight I was cross-referencing digests and noting-up cases. By 2 a.m., the words on the screen had begun to swim. I'd found three potentially relevant cases, but their facts were distinguishable. The panic was no longer a feeling; it was a chemical taste in my mouth, like sucking on a battery. At 3:17 a.m., I found it: a Court of Appeal decision from St John's that was, against all odds, directly on point. The rush of triumph was physical, a wave of heat across my shoulders. I printed it, my hand trembling.

In 1993-1994, we had to pull real books off real shelves. Most of our work came by voicemail. Email, newly introduced, landed on our screen like a black anvil smashing your work, disrupting your momentum, scornful of any urgency, and demanding you respond before resuming your task. When emails started catching on, they would ruin our day about once every twenty seconds.

Despite everything, the memo was on Carson's desk by 8:50 a.m. He walked past my office at 10:15 a.m., barely breaking his stride.

"Got it," he said. No eye contact. No "thank you." Just two syllables that meant you may continue to exist here, but don't unpack your bags yet.

Weeks later, a different partner admonished me for citing Newfoundland case law, maintaining that even an articling student should know that no sober judge in Ontario would follow Newfoundland's jurisprudence, even though his own sobriety was occasionally questioned. It felt as though I was meant to be a mind reader, punished for my inability to divine intentions. Impossible standards had to be met to succeed.

The billing sheets, or dockets, as we called them, fell on the moral divide between theory and sacrament. Every day we accounted for our six-minute increments, each 0.1 representing a tenth of an hour. "Research re: NL limitation periods – 4.2 hours." "Draft memo – 1.8 hours," a deliberate underestimation of the time spent to avoid appearing incompetent. As a moral document, the docket sheet remained ambivalent. Did I bill for the seven minutes I stared at the wall, brain empty? Did I bill for the bathroom break? I learned to bill for both and reduce later. Survival was a rounding error based on underdeveloped instincts of how long assignments should take. For every lawyer who ever delegated a task to a student, the task was a simple one; it should be done immediately and should not take more than 2 hours.

In the angled corridors of the golden tower of Bay Street, competition remained a silent current beneath everything. We were twenty-five distinct species of fear, although some disguised it better than others.

There was Mark, the natural. His father was a client. He used terms like "debenture" and "prospectus" in casual conversation, as if discussing the weather. He wore ties that looked soft and expensive. He never seemed to sweat.

My secret ally was a senior associate, five years ahead of me in the trenches. He was the one who translated partner instructions into plain language in late-night bursts in the binding room, who passed the industrial stapler back and forth without speaking.

Once, near midnight, I found him standing still in a silent stairwell, staring at the wall. His face was a mask of pure fatigue. He took a long, shuddering breath that seemed to come from the soles of his shoes, straightened his tie, and walked back toward the light without a word. Within months, he was gone.

The official story curtly presented him as pursuing opportunities elsewhere with a perfunctory thank you for his many contributions. The unofficial story moved between floors in lowered voices: a critical deadline missed on a file run by a notoriously unclear partner;

the blame somehow sliding off its proper target onto a convenient associate; another partner raising his voice, insisting, wrongly, that this was the man at fault. In the spirit of *every-mistake-needs-a-scape-goat,* Bay Street had done what Weber Street excelled at: reassigning responsibility to the body most available.

It was my first close-up view of how a system could dispense with someone decent, not because he was incompetent, but because he was in the wrong place when the music stopped.

Sometime in the first six months, my articling principal, an esteemed litigator and senior partner whose name carried the quiet heft of precedent, summoned me for my first performance evaluation. His office was larger than my apartment. He sat behind a vast desk, surrounded on three sides by floor-to-ceiling glass. The northern Toronto skyline sprawled before him, a panorama of achieved ambition; the angled glass expertly shielded him from the sun's jarring brilliance. I sat in the client chair, thinking that his career, his office, his reputation was everything I had ever wanted and dared to dream was possible.

He looked at me with practiced inscrutability and delivered the preliminary verdict. I tried too hard. I was too intense. I should stop asking litigators for more work; they already knew where my interests lay. Stop giving unsolicited progress reports. Nobody wanted a play-by-play.

Then, using a word unknown to me, he offered the closest thing to a compliment I would receive. He said I possessed an "infrangible gravity."

I held my breath the whole time. I could see his lips moving but could no longer hear the words. When I left the room, with no real sense of the quality of my work, only the shape of my flaws, my breath returned in a slow, controlled leak. A tension headache ignited behind my eyes, a low-grade fire that would burn for hours.

I went straight to the library, to the heavy, cloth-bound Oxford dictionary on the wooden stand normally reserved for Blackstone's

Commentaries on the Laws of England. My fingers fumbled through the thin pages, fighting a gathering storm in my chest.

Infrangible: unbreakable. That which cannot be shattered. Gravity: weight. Seriousness. Solemnity.

Infrangible gravity.

To the partners and associates of McMillan Binch, the people who mattered most in that moment of my life, I was not a lawyer in the making. I was not a protégé—let alone a prodigy. I was something far less, as my mother always knew and loved to say. I was an itinerant rainstorm: *Chief Dark Cloud.*

From that day on, I learned to perform "less intense." I wasn't going to let my intensity darken their doors or rain on their files anymore. I would be easier, lighter, and smoother. I could learn the part, if it kept me in the tower.

But the city has its own way of reading you, especially at night, when the costume starts to slip.

Chapter 18

Subway Wisdom

> *At any street corner the feeling of absurdity can strike any man in the face.*
>
> — Albert Camus, *The Myth of Sisyphus*

ON LATE NIGHTS at McMillan Binch, it sometimes felt safer to take the short subway ride from Union Station to Dundas. I was articling at a golden tower at the southernmost corner of Bay at Front Street, but living at 40 Gerrard Street East, past the Eaton Centre at the northern boundary of Toronto Metropolitan University (formerly Ryerson University). In the mid-nineties, odd things were known to happen in the wee hours after the lawyers and investment bankers went home.

One such night, I found myself riding a mostly empty train, suit rumpled, tie loosened, manspreading by the doors like any young man trying to disguise anxiety as comfort. Across the aisle sat a man about my age, disheveled, likely homeless, wearing a stained baby blue hoodie covering a gray T-shirt that drooped over Scooby-Doo pajama bottoms. Light brown hair fell unkempt under his hood and over his forehead. He was staring at me. And he was angry.

It wasn't performative rage or incoherent muttering. It was a cold, locked-on, teeth-clenched fury. I didn't know him, but I recognized the expression. Anger mixed with something deeper and older, resentment spiked with shame.

I avoided eye contact. Six, maybe seven minutes passed. Two stops. Queen Station loomed.

He stood. We locked eyes.

I straightened, not aggressively, just enough to signal I was ready. I was a competitive wrestler in high school. More importantly, I grew up on Weber Street. I knew I could take a punch.

As the subway eased into Queen, he took one step backward, then another, holding the door open with one hand and his gaze with the other. Then, with the slow, deliberate cadence of a Clint Eastwood line reading, he said, pointing at me: "Your Head. Is. Too Big. For. Your Body." And he stepped off.

The doors closed. The train pulled away. Someone laughed that short, shocked laugh you let out when something has startled you but left you unharmed. Another chuckled. The moment expanded. We laughed, strangers now bonded by an unexpected and perfect insult.

I smiled. *He's not wrong*, I thought.

The next morning, I'd put the suit back on, re-loop the tie, and ride the elevator back into a world where the real threat wasn't a subway confrontation, it was being found out. The man at Queen Station had said something absurd, but it stuck with me. *Of course, my head is too big*, I thought. *Why else would I be here?*

That night, and every night that winter, I would come home after midnight and drop face-down onto the futon, knees still on the floor. I would try to pray but found nothing to say. The sharp, level sounds of a sleepless city went unnoticed as my mind occupied itself with only two thoughts: the firm's hire back decision, expected in May, and my desire to die before morning. Exhaustion would eventually overcome the second thought and push me toward sleep until, always too soon, the morning broke.

Those dark, persistent thoughts were enough to make me visit a walk-in medical clinic. After fifteen minutes of listing symptoms, I walked out with a self-renewing six-month supply of Prozac for the depression and Imovane for sleep. The sleep medication helped. The antidepressant didn't. None ever would. But with some sleep I could work, and work distracted me from the depression, and so the loop continued: the office, the subway, the dark apartment, the city sounds, the thoughts, and finally the Imovane doing its job.

The next day, I bought a flight to Paris to coincide with my last day of articling. I told myself I was going to decompress. Really, I was waiting for an answer, for a signal, for permission to finally believe I belonged.

Chapter 19

The Decision

> *You need not leave your room. Remain sitting at your table and listen. You need not even listen, simply wait. You need not even wait, just learn to become quiet and still, and solitary. The world will freely offer itself to you to be unmasked.*
>
> — Franz Kafka

The hire back decision became the sun we orbited, unseen but inescapable. It was the moment articling students learned their future, the anxious conclusion to twelve months of tirelessly trying to impress everyone all the time. If successful, we would have jobs to come back to in January 1995, with careers launched from the prestigious platform McMillian Binch provided. Failure meant intolerable uncertainty about whether you could you find work; what kind of firm would hire you; what kind of law practice would accept you; whether completing a Master of Laws made more sense; where would you go; how would you support yourself in the meantime... Would I have to return to Weber Street?

Our articling term ran through the fall, into the dead of winter and early spring. By the end of May 1994, we were supposed to be told our fates.

May came and went without a word. By June we had all dispersed for the summer, our fates technically undecided but practically sealed. I joined friends for a summer in France, spending the savings I thought of as an advance on a future that was already mine.

It was not.

On Friday, 17 June 1994, the phone rang in the place where I was staying in France. The voice from Toronto was polite, almost apologetic. I would not be invited back. I was not among the six. They only needed one new associate in litigation. I had come second.

In that moment, the frame shifted again. I was suddenly a man in a foreign country, spending savings he now needed, with no job awaiting his return. The Rheon line at Weston Bakeries and its merciless oven, the pan-thumper station, flickered back into view as a possible future.

That same day, cameras followed a white Ford Bronco down a Los Angeles freeway at low speed, broadcasting O.J. Simpson's crisis into living rooms and bars and airport lounges across North America and around the world.

In Rwanda, hundreds of thousands had already been murdered in a genocide most of the world barely noticed, as tens of thousands of bodies, scattered throughout the small, mountainous heart of Africa.

In Bosnia, the war ground on, a brutal and relentless struggle. The planet was on fire in several places at once, not unlike today.

I didn't understand it fully then, but the pattern was familiar, of systems that punish the wrong people. Attention lavished on the wrong crises. Political frameworks that made certain harms seem invisible, and certain lives feel expendable, especially the ones already convinced they are.

At twenty-six, I retreated to a new rail-spur clearing. After I had made the circle of all the major tourist sites, I found a bench in Luxembourg Gardens near the Latin Quarter in Paris. I barely moved for three weeks, taking a break only to walk to nearby Saint-Sulpice where, at dusk, I stumbled upon a pipe-organ rehearsal in the heart of the cathedral.

I had brought books from my father's secret library with me, the ones I had discovered in his closet, days before he died in February 1988. In the city where he had lived between 1954 and 1967, where he had read poetry in Italian and philosophy in French, and loved the works of Balzac, Proust, Hugo, after whom my brother Victor is named, I opened the books he had kept in his fifth language and my first. In that time and in that place, I connected with my father in ways that were not possible when he was alive.

A Tale of Two Cities landed hard and left its imprimatur. I read of Sydney Carton, the dissipated, brilliant man who sacrificed himself at the guillotine so that the woman he loved could be with the man she loved. It was a story of wasted potential redeemed by a single, final act of meaning.

But it was a different passage that locked itself into my bones, a description that seemed to have been waiting for me in that park, in that summer, with that phone call still ringing in my ears: "Sadly, sadly, the sun rose. It rose upon no sadder sight than the man of good abilities and good emotions, incapable of their directed exercise, incapable of his own help or happiness, sensible about the blight upon him and resigning himself to let it eat him away."

I read it once. Then again. I didn't just memorize the words. I couldn't forget them. I closed the book and sat still, in the metal chair shaded by trees that encircled the Medici Fountain on the eastern side of the gardens. The words adhered to me with the force of a diagnosis. The man of good abilities... incapable of their directed exercise... sensible about the blight upon him and resigning himself to let it eat him away.

This described Sydney Carton before his redemptive self-sacrifice. His life before confronting the guillotine. This was the prophecy my articling principal had unknowingly pronounced: infrangible gravity. A weight that could not be broken, only carried. A blight you were sensible of but resigned to accept. It read less like literature and more like a road map to the kind of man who, one day, might call his own self-sacrificing disappearance an act of love.

I sat in my father's city, holding my father's book, and understood with a clarity that was almost peaceful: Dickens had just revealed the man I was becoming.

Back in Toronto, the tower still stood; its glass was unbroken. The articling students who had been chosen would walk through their doors in January as junior lawyers, slightly higher in the food chain, slightly less replaceable. I would walk into something else entirely.

The frame, the structure of expectation, fear, and silent judgment that held this gleaming life in place, was no longer something I merely looked at. It was something I was both inside and suddenly outside of. I imagined pressing my hand against the cool, unbreakable glass of the tower in my mind and feeling, beneath my palm, the faint vibration of a different truth.

Chapter 20

The Red Tower

> *I returned, and saw under the sun, that the race is not to the swift, nor the battle to the strong, neither yet bread to the wise, nor yet riches to men of understanding, nor yet favour to men of skill; but time and chance happeneth to them all.*
>
> — Ecclesiastes 9:11, KJV

THE CLARITY I'd found in Luxembourg Gardens lasted exactly as long as the money in my bank account. The first thing to go was Paris. The second was my apartment.

With nothing but a suitcase, a few books, and an articling salary about to expire, I did what every terrified, overeducated twenty-six-year-old dreads: I moved back home to Weber Street.

The house had not improved with age. The siding sagged. The front steps tilted, as if leaning away from their own foundation. Inside, the day care had evolved from a noisy occupation into a full occupation force. Toddlers moved in packs, sticky-fingered and loud, leaving plastic landmines in every walkway.

The newest additions were two uncaged cockatoos: Chubby and Pearl. They lived on a metal stand in the living room, white feathers and yellow crests, their black eyes sharp with judgment. When the children shrieked, the birds shrieked back, a call-and-response of chaos. Their droppings ringed the base of their perch like a chalk outline. Occasionally they launched into looping flights around the main floor, landing on curtain rods and picture frames, leaving their white signatures wherever they pleased.

I slept again in my old room, the air thick with bleach and soiled diapers, cartoons murmuring through the walls. At night, when the house finally fell quiet, I could hear the soft shuffle of cockatoo feet on metal and the occasional clink of beak on cage. I had left Bay Street and Paris and returned to the place where my mind had first been taught its worth.

Every weekday began before five in the morning. I dressed in the blue glow of my alarm clock, slipped out into the damp Kitchener air, and walked to the Charles Street Transit Terminal, past shuttered storefronts and childhood streets, now in a suit and overcoat, briefcase in hand.

At the terminal, the Greyhound bus idled in the dark with its familiar diesel shudder. Among factory workers, students, nurses, we filed on in silence, each calculating what time, money, and hope we could still afford to spend.

The route to Toronto was 113 kilometres of negotiated survival. On good days, the ride took two and a half hours. On bad ones, when snow swallowed the 401, it could take four.

By eight-thirty or nine, depending on traffic and luck, I'd surface into the light at Union Station, then walk north toward interviews, bar admission classes, and the remnants of a plan. Every morning, I passed through the golden foyer of the Royal Bank Plaza, the building that had once offered me a future and then retracted it. I didn't need to go that way, but I went anyway. Inside, the new associates would soon begin their careers. I was outside, walking north.

To their credit, McMillan Binch paid full salaries to all articling students, whether we were hired back or not. That cheque bought me a few extra months which equated to bus tickets, bar admission fees, groceries for the day care, and time to find work without immediately surrendering to the Rheon line.

Bay Street was still gripped by recession. Firms were trimming partnerships, shrinking summer classes, hiring almost no one. There was no space for outliers.

The problem wasn't just the competition. It was the architecture. Each firm filled its entry-level positions with its own articling students, the ones who had already survived their own controlled burns. No firm needed to draft someone else's orphan.

My résumé said one thing: top grades, law review, articled at a major Bay Street firm. But my file said something else: not hired back. In this small world, that single line carried its own quiet accusation: What's wrong with him?

The one person who could shift the narrative was my articling principal. In our final meeting, he told me I should be "commended for appearing less intense," as though I were a violinist being congratulated for playing more softly. Still, he offered something invaluable: letters to half a dozen senior litigators at other firms.

The letters worked. Interviews arrived like small, wary birds. I sat in reception areas up and down Bay Street, watching associates glide past with the casual ease of those who knew where the bathrooms were. I modulated my story: not "I was cut," but "McMillan only hired one student in litigation this year." Not "I moved back to Weber Street," but "I'm commuting from Kitchener while I finish bar admission." I spoke in fluent understatement and hoped no one could smell the Greyhound diesel on my suit.

One interview was at Borden & Elliot. The firm occupied seven floors of Scotia Plaza, thirty-four through thirty-nine, and forty-one. Where the Royal Bank glittered in gold and glass, Scotia Plaza stood deep burgundy, clad in polished Imperial Red granite. The building caught the sun like something pulled from the earth under pressure.

Inside, an eleven-storey atrium opened like a lung: marble floors, fountains, palm trees. Lawyers and bankers moved through the space with the soft hush of power. The tower rose in tiers above them, crowned by a green glass pyramid that glowed at night like a beacon. From the sidewalk, it was impossible not to look up and think this is what success looks like.

The interview was a blur of boardrooms, water glasses, and polite questions. I remember being asked why I wanted to be a litigator, as if the answer weren't obvious: because it was the only place where words and rules could protect someone other than myself. I said something about fairness. About advocacy. The partner nodded, like he'd heard it all before.

Then came silence. Weeks passed. The Greyhound rides continued. The letters had done their work. Now all I could do was wait. I applied to government jobs, in-house roles, anything with "legal" in the description.

At Weber Street, the day care carried on. Chubby and Pearl screamed their commentary. I watched the calendar crawl toward Christmas with the dread of a man waiting for disappointment but needing to perform happy.

The call came on Friday December 23, 1994. I was in the kitchen, slouched in a chair, staring at my hands, and resisting the temptation to despair, when the phone rang. My mother answered, then handed it to me with the look she reserved for news that was either money or disaster.

The voice on the line was calm, raspy, and unflinchingly professional. A partner from Borden & Elliot. They were pleased to offer me a position as a first-year associate in litigation, starting next month. Salary: $58,000, the equivalent of $110,600 today.

I thanked him with the restraint I hoped sounded equally professional, hung up, and stepped into the narrow hallway. Chubby and Pearl watched from their perch, cocked to one side, as if weighing whether to approve.

In the year of mass layoffs and record-low hire back numbers, I had somehow been plucked from the pool of undrafted free agents and invited back into the game, this time by one of the most prestigious firms in the country.

On the third of January in 1995, I stepped into Scotia Plaza as a Borden & Elliot associate. I rode the elevator up with a crowd of strangers, all smelling faintly of coffee, fried egg sandwiches, and bodywash. Outside the elevator, red granite slid past unseen.

Inside me, something heavier slid into place. My career was back on track. But gravity—old, familiar, unrelenting—was already waiting at the top.

Chapter 21

The Palace

> *In a real dark night of the soul, it is always three o'clock in the morning.*
>
> — F. Scott Fitzgerald, *The Crack-Up (1936)*

FROM THE OUTSIDE, the story held. I was a first-year associate at one of the country's most prestigious firms. I walked each morning into the red granite tower. I billed, I argued, I learned to stand at the counsel table without shaking. The boy from Weber Street and its cockatoos had become a litigator in the very heart of Bay Street.

And, somewhere in that ascent, I reunited with Jelena. I had known her since 1987 when we were both nineteen-year-old students at the University of Waterloo enrolled in the same program. Unlike me, Jelena completed her undergraduate degree before starting a four-year joint JD and MBA program at the University of Toronto. This meant that she would become a lawyer in 1997, two years after me.

Jelena was everything the profession admired and much that it had no language to describe. She was intelligent, disciplined, funny in a dry way that cut through my veneer of self-importance and two years of "seniority." We laughed easily and often at the same things; mostly at feeling like misfits in a world where fitting in meant everything.

She had grown up in a different universe than Weber Street. One with stability, dinner tables that did not explode, conversations that did not crackle with unspoken threats. She carried herself with a kind of ease and intelligent sophistication I mistook for invulnerability.

She also carried her own weather. When I would later reflect on our shared history, which I did often in later years, I would wonder whether it was ever wise for two lawyers to marry, let alone two anxious and depressed ones.

By the time we became engaged, in May 1995, about eighteen months after we reconnected, I knew she was struggling. Anxiety shadowed her. Self-doubt stalked her in ways that looked painfully familiar. That spring, while we were engaged, she departed for a thirty-seven-day guided tour of Europe with Contiki, a tour outfit that served eighteen to thirty-five year olds. During that trip, she started an affair.

The facts are simple; the feelings were not. I found out and we tried to repair it. I could have walked away. Instead, I reached for the story I understood best: if I could love someone hard enough, steadily enough, unconditionally enough, they would eventually learn to love themselves, and, almost as an afterthought, me.

It was not a logical decision. It was a faith statement. It was also the way I wanted to be loved.

Jelena and I were married on Saturday August 17, 1996. The wedding had all the markers of a happy beginning: formal invitations, rented tuxedos, relatives rounded up and made temporarily presentable. My mother-in-law fussed over flowers. My mother beamed with pride as if our wedding redeemed hers. She lobbied hard and got what she considered was a proper wedding in a Roman Catholic Church. My father, gone now for over eight years, made his presence felt by his absence, in the pauses between speeches, the toast to the bride he could not utter, and the rare photos we included in our video montage set to Celine Dion's hit "Because You Loved Me."

I stood at the front of the church in a black tuxedo as Jelena walked toward me in white and watched the familiar split-screen in my mind. On one side, the scene everyone else saw was a smiling couple at the start of their life. On the other, the commentary track from Weber Street: Are you sure you belong here? Do you know what you're doing? How long before they find out?

At the Holy Name of Mary Church in Windsor, I said the words. I slipped the ring on her finger and, together, we listened to the longest, most excruciating homily ever delivered in the history of the Catholic church. I kissed her in front of friends and colleagues, and for a moment the voice inside me went quiet.

We moved into a condominium at 1 Palace Place, on the thirty-eighth floor, a tower on the Etobicoke waterfront that rose over Lake Ontario like a cruise ship anchored in concrete. From our windows, the city glittered in the distance, the CN Tower a thin needle against the sky. On clear mornings, the lake lay flat and metallic; on stormy nights, the wind hurled itself against the glass and reminded us that we were suspended thirty-eight floors above the ground in a very small box.

For a boy who had shared a bedroom in a house that vibrated whenever a truck drove by, the elevator ride alone felt like a promotion. The lobby had marble floors and a concierge. There was a gym and a pool under a glass cathedral. The hallways were quiet. No children crashed through the doors with runny noses and untied shoelaces. No birds screamed from a perch. It was, in every sense, a palace.

We bought dishes that matched. We stocked our fridge with more than baking soda. On weekends, we walked the lakeshore, watching small planes lift off from the Island Airport. Sometimes we took the streetcar downtown to meet friends, easing ourselves into the lives we thought we were supposed to have.

I was learning, badly and slowly, how to be a husband. It is not a skill the law teaches. There is no bar course for listening without cross-examining, no practice direction for admitting fear without turning it into anger. At work, my job was to know, to diagnose, to argue, to sound certain. At home, that instinct followed me. Rather than say I was scared or overwhelmed, I would explain. I built arguments where what was needed was confession.

Jelena was finding her own way through the marriage. She was fiercely independent and rightly proud of the career she had built. She insisted on asserting that independence in our home, on not becoming, as she put it, "someone's domestic help." Dishes and laundry and cleaning became small flashpoints, not because of the tasks themselves but because of what they symbolized. She could be sharply critical of herself and of me, sometimes comparing me unfavorably to other men or lawyers we both knew, as though trying to calibrate some internal scale she did not trust.

We were two wounded people trying to build a shared life on top of old foundations neither of us fully understood nor properly repaired. From the outside, we looked like a successful Bay Street couple in a glass tower on the lake. Inside, there were already hairline cracks.

At the firm, I was being trained by some of the best trial lawyers in the country. They let me stand beside them, then slightly in front of them, then finally alone. I learned how to build a case from a banker's box of unsorted documents, how to cross-examine without losing the judge, how to read the minute tilt of a judge's head. I learned that sometimes the most powerful thing you can do is not to win, but to make sure your client's story is heard.

In June 1999, our daughter, Candace, was born. There was no generous parental leave then, no template for how a Bay Street associate might be both present at home and indispensable at work. I was in the middle of a factum for the Ontario Court of Appeal. While Jelena slept in the hospital bed, pale and emptied by labor, I sat in the visitor's chair beside her, alternating between staring at this impossible new human in the bassinet and typing submissions under the glow of a bedside lamp.

Relief arrived first: she was alive, breathing, whole. Joy came in increments, the weight of her in my arms; the way her fingers wrapped around my little finger with unreasonable force; the way her face settled when she heard my voice.

At night, back at Palace Place, she made her needs known the way newborns do, with full-throated cries that sliced through walls and sleep. I got up with her as often as I could, padding across the dark bedroom, lifting her from the crib, feeling the heat of her small body against my chest.

I would stand at the window, looking out over the city lights and the black sheet of the lake, and rock her gently. Her crying would soften into hiccups, then into small, sleepy breaths. In those moments, the courtroom, the red tower, the deadlines all fell away. It was just the two of us in a box of light above the water.

Almost every night, I sang the same song, "You Are My Sunshine," into the soft spot above her ear.

The words felt almost embarrassingly on-the-nose, but they were true in a way few things in my life had ever felt true. I meant every syllable. Please don't take my sunshine away.

I swore, in those midnight hours, that I would not become my father. I would not make love contingent on performance. I would not turn my daughter into a receptacle for my shame. It was a sincere promise. But it was not a cure.

Depression does not care about vows. It is indifferent to job titles, palaces, and black-tie events. It coexists quite comfortably with competence. In those years in the red tower and the palace on the lake, I was learning to be a lawyer, a husband, and a father at the same time.

Chapter 22

The Partner

> *What shall it profit a man, if he shall gain the whole world, and lose his own soul?*
>
> — Mark 8:36 KJV

By the turn of the millennium, the crack in the glass was no longer invisible. If you stood close enough, you could see it.

I was exactly where a Bay Street associate was supposed to be four and a half years in. I had my own files, my own clients, my own crop of students to send to the binding room at midnight. I could walk into most Toronto courthouses without checking the floor directory. Judges knew my name well enough. Inside the firm, people had started to say "partner" in the same sentence as my own.

At home, the palace was adrift and listing.

Jelena's panic attack in February 1999 had taken her out of the workforce and deposited her, dazed and wounded, back into our living room. Her file at the firm went quiet. Her name slipped off the lists. In our condo, she was painfully present.

She had wrapped much of her identity around her work. Without it, her floor dropped away. Anxiety moved from background noise to foreground. Small decisions became cross-examinations. Where my response to pressure was to work more, hers was to freeze and then blame herself for freezing. We were two nervous systems locked in a tragic embrace, triggering each other's alarms.

I tried to be understanding. I took on more of the earning, more of the practical load, more of the emotional translation. I told myself this was what unconditional love looked like: you carry more when the other person can't. You don't complain about the weight. But there are weights you can't out-argue.

The affair during our engagement had never fully left the room. It sat between us in certain arguments, in certain long silences. Jelena's criticisms, sharpened by her own self-disgust, sometimes landed directly on me.

We loved each other. We were also wearing each other out. By the summer of 2000, something in me had run dry.

Love, I had been taught, was a choice, a verb. Work at it and you could keep it alive. What no one tells you is that choices are made by human beings with finite reserves. You cannot indefinitely pour from a well that isn't being refilled. You can tell yourself a story about being the stronger one, the rescuer, the one who will absorb the damage. But eventually your body, your mind, your heart start sending back a different answer.

In August 2000, standing in a pool at the Barcelo Mayo Resort near Tulum, Mexico, I heard myself say words I had not rehearsed but could not silence for many months.

"I don't love you anymore," I told Jelena. "I think we need to separate." She looked at me with bland indifference, folding Candace in her arms, and simply said: "You never did." There was no shouting, anger, or insults. Just acceptance, as if we had arrived at our inevitable end. Gratefully, our vacation also ended the next day.

There is no clean way to end a marriage, but there are especially messy ways. Ours was one of them. Shock gave way to anger; anger gave way to negotiations; negotiations gave way to lawyers. We were two people in pain, with different stories about who had been hurt more, asking the law to adjudicate what the human heart could not resolve.

Divorce is a machine. You feed it money, time, affidavits, and it grinds slowly toward orders that are never as satisfying as anyone imagines. It does not pause to consider that both parties may be carrying old injuries into the ring. It does not ask if either of you can emotionally afford the process. It simply moves.

To finance that movement, our palace had to be sold. Palace Place, with its marble lobby and lake view and elevator that had once felt like a promotion, went on the market. Boxes appeared. Walls emptied. Our thirty-eighth-floor home shed the evidence that we had ever lived there. It was not just a real-estate transaction; it was a public notice that the frame we had tried to build together had cracked beyond repair.

The proceeds would not make us rich. By the time legal fees, debts, and the economics of two households were accounted for, the divorce would, in time, bankrupt me. The boy who had fled Weber Street for the golden tower, and then the red one, was heading back down the highway toward Kitchener.

But before that, there was another blow.

In mid-December 2000, Jelena took Candace to Windsor.

It was a move made in the context of our separation and custody disputes, but the effect was brutally simple: my daughter, my only sunshine, was now several hours down the highway, in another city, living a life apart from me. Until the court could hear the matter and make orders about access, I would not see her. The first available date was not until May 2001, six months later.

Between that December and the spring, my contact with Candace was limited to the phone and my imagination. I pictured her in unfamiliar rooms, hearing the story of our family from only one side. Toddlers have short memories, the experts say. Fathers don't. Each missed weekend landed in my chest with the weight of a verdict.

Two weeks after they left, the firm made me a partner. On January 1, 2001, my name went up on the partnership list. I was alone in a half-packed condo on the lake, my tiny family in a different city, when the official letter arrived. At the office the next day, there was a framed announcement, a handshake, a few congratulations. I smiled, thanked people, and went back to my desk to docket my time. I had never been more depressed.

While it might have looked like a triumph for the boy from Weber Street, now a partner at a major Bay Street firm, it felt like being pinned to a board. The partnership letter felt like a demanding expectation, rather than a promotion. I felt proud, grateful, and anxious, but I never felt happy. The joy I once felt coursing through me as I read my admission letter to University of Toronto's Law program seemed impossible to remember or summon. It was replaced with anticipatory exhaustion arising from far greater expectations, the omnipresent fear of hushed ridicule in partners' meetings, and the heavy financial toll of spousal support and child support.

In May 2001, I finally saw my daughter again in a courtroom, the setting I least wanted for her. We sat in the reception areas, as our lawyers argued before a judge, using the sanitized legal frame of "the best interests of the child" over whether and how often a father could see his daughter. I had spent years advocating for clients in courtrooms and conference rooms, speaking about fairness, justice, and best interests. Now I stood on the other side of the bar, my own life subject to the measured tone of a stranger whose authority loomed over me. I smirked to myself at the thought that, if you count Jelena, me, our counsel, and the judge, there were five lawyers trying to resolve a simple issue.

Predictable court orders were made. I would see Candace again, not as often as I wanted, but more than not at all. Jelena's self-avowed absence of empathy made me want full custody, but I was told with the stern authority only a judge can deliver, that children belong with their mothers, not their fathers. I will always regret that I didn't fight harder and longer.

By the end of June, the sale of Palace Place closed. Whatever remained, after the divorce machinery took its share, went into an old house in Kitchener.

On June 30, 2001, at thirty-three, I moved into 136 Young Street. If Weber Street had been my childhood cathedral of shame, Young Street was a kind of annex, close enough to visit the past, but far enough to pretend I had left it.

With Young Street came the Greyhound again. The commute I thought I had left behind in 1994 returned in a more bitter form. Before five each morning, I was back on the streets of Kitchener in a suit, briefcase in hand, walking toward the bus terminal, as the thirty-something partner version of the twenty-five-year-old articling student. I had more responsibility, more weight, but the same diesel smell.

During the day, I worked the punishing hours of Bay Street litigation. At night, I came home to motions, emails, and the small explosions that happen in a house where three generations would soon be learning new rhythms.

Weekends with Candace were gifts wrapped in exhaustion. I strapped her into a car seat, drove to parks and playgrounds, and read *Harry Potter* in a voice that sometimes shook with more than fatigue.

One night, after putting Candace to bed during a weekend visit, I stood in the dark kitchen and did the math. My life insurance payout would cover her university tuition, pay off my mother's debts, and leave Jelena financially secure. The math was cleaner than any argument I'd ever drafted. For the first time, my death looked less like tragedy and more like estate planning, and that frightened me less than it should have.

The frame of my life had never looked stronger. I made partner, was a homeowner, a father, and a dutiful son. But the glass had never felt more fragile.

By the end of December 1859, Dickens had described the "man of good abilities and good emotions, incapable of their directed exercise, incapable of his own help or happiness." Sitting on the Greyhound in the dark, my name newly inscribed on a brass plate affixed to one of the corner offices reserved for partners, my daughter asleep in another city, my mother in the spare room at Young Street, I began to understand the man with greater clarity. I had overcome Sister Eleanor's labels, fulfilled Mrs. Forester's early faith, and achieved everything I was supposed to want, only to feel numbed by it all.

The gravity that had followed me from Weber Street to Bay Street, from the golden tower to the red one, was no longer a background force. It was the main story. It pulled at my work, my relationships, my sense of myself as a father. It whispered, with increasing confidence, that everyone around me would be better off if I were not here to fail them.

Chapter 23

The Second Palace

> *The past is never dead. It's not even past.*
>
> — William Faulkner, *Requiem for a Nun*

YOUNG STREET WAS SUPPOSED to be a correction. The first had been Palace Place, a glass tower on the Etobicoke waterfront, suspended above Lake Ontario, where my first marriage ended and my divorce began. The move back to Kitchener in 2001, to a house at 136 Young Street, felt like an attempt to rebuild something sturdier at ground level, closer to where I had started, and far enough from the lake that the floor didn't feel like it could drop away at any moment.

The house at 136 was nothing like the square little boxes that filled most of Kitchener's side streets. It was a 1929 arts-and-crafts place, stone and stucco, perched on the corner across from Hibner Park, a twenty-minute walk from my mother's house at 282 Weber. The rooflines were odd and appealing. The ceilings were high. The bones were beautiful and tired.

It was also a collection of small disasters. The copper eavestroughs were elegant and leaking. The wiring was knob-and-tube, the sort of thing that made electricians shake their heads before naming a price. The back deck was rotting in slow motion. Buried under the front porch was an undisclosed, unserviced oil tank, an environmental violation I only discovered two years later when a buyer's home inspector pointed it out. In the basement, the main load-bearing pillars were wrapped in asbestos, as if the house were clinging to an earlier century's idea of progress.

The whole structure was about twelve hundred square feet. Three bedrooms: one for me, one for my mother, and one for Candace when she stayed with us. From the street, it looked like a modest house in a good location. Inside, it felt like living withing a beautiful wound—charm, danger, conflict, unmet expectations, and deferred maintenance all under one roof.

My mother still lived at 282 Weber when I bought my house. Weber itself had changed and remained unchanged. The day care was still there, the zoo of toddlers still in full shriek. Two doors down, as it had been since the early 1980s, roared the Hells Angels motorcycle club. Where children once rode tricycles, tattooed men in leather leaned against chrome bikes, engines rumbling, rock music concussing the street. The neighbors called themselves "Angels," but the ambient tension felt like Hell.

When 136 Young became real and I had keys in my hand and a mortgage approved, the thought that rose first was not just about my own escape. It was that I could rescue my mother from Weber. So, I asked her to move in, bring Chubby and Pearl, her dog Justice, and slowly but deliberately, retire the day care.

Although my lawyer implored me to reconsider living with my mother, the decision made sense from most angles. Young Street was minutes away from 282 Weber by car, twenty minutes on foot, but felt like another town. Hibner Park sat across the street with its trees and playground, a softer horizon than the biker clubhouse. When I had Candace on weekends, my mother could help with baths and bedtime. Sharing costs would make everything easier. It could be a fresh start for both of us.

She agreed. We moved her life to a short but symbolic distance from 282 to 136, including day care toys and furniture, the familiar couches, and the boxes of things she'd kept long after my father died.

Hells Angels stayed behind at 278 and 280. I remember standing in her emptied living room at Weber, the indentations in the carpet where the TV and couch had been, thinking, *Finally, she doesn't have to live next to Hell anymore.*

But nostalgia and regret hit my mother like a punch to the face. She fell to the floor of her empty house and sobbed. Walter and I grabbed an arm each and gently walked her to the truck outside. I had underestimated how much Hell we both carried inside us.

At Young Street, the geography changed; the choreography did not. My mother brought the habits that had kept her upright at Weber, like vigilance, criticism, and a thrifty suspicion of anything that looked like comfort. I brought my own over-responsibility, apologies, and a readiness to believe I was still disappointing her.

We fell back into familiar positions with almost no effort. If something in the house went wrong, and things in that house went wrong regularly, it became another proof that I had made a bad decision. If I worked late in Toronto and came back exhausted, it became another example of how I was never quite doing enough at home. I loved her. She loved me. We were also exhausting each other in ways that we had rehearsed since childhood.

My brother Walter added another layer to the geography of our family story when he and his family moved into the old home at 282 Weber, next door to the Hells Angels clubhouse that still roared in the evenings. The street that had formed us swallowed one of us again.

When I drove between Young and Weber, it felt like passing between chapters of the same book that refused to close. We could move in and out, but the house would never leave. Neither would its secrets.

I had written our old neighbor Steve and his family into my memory as a sanctuary. He was the unlocked door, the Econoline, the camping trips, a father figure whose hand never rose in anger. For twenty years, that story held. It was the one bright clearing in the undergrowth of Weber Street; the chapter I could tell without wincing.

I don't remember exactly when I learned the truth, only that it arrived the way most revelations about childhood do, as a series of quiet corrections that rearranged everything I thought I knew. Steve's departure from Weber Street was not voluntary. He was forced out by my aunt and mother. The reasons were darker than a child could understand, and they involved the abuse of someone I loved. I will not say more, because the story is not mine alone to tell. But the man I had mourned as a lost father figure was not the man I believed him to be. The hole in the world I could not patch had been cut by hands I had trusted.

When I was about twelve, Steve invited me to his bedroom to see something forbidden. He darkened the room and projected an 8 mm film onto his bare eggshell-white wall. The chatter-chatter-chatter filled the room as the wall displayed monstrous images of a short pornographic film. It was graphic, shocking, and utterly beyond my comprehension. Steve didn't force me to watch it. He didn't have to. I was too starved for adult attention and inclusion to leave his side. I still see those images forty-seven years later, not as memory but as residue—sharp, unwelcome, permanently etched.

I did not understand then what I understand now; that the warmth and the invitation were part of the same intention; that what felt like inclusion was also preparation; that the man who gave a needy boy attention knew exactly what he was doing.

Steve is dead now. I have carried these facts for decades, too ashamed to utter them, as though the shame belonged to me rather than the man who earned it. I include them here not to revise the comfort I felt as a child, because that comfort was real and needed by a credulous boy unable to understand, let alone appreciate, its mendacious purpose. I name it now but because a memoir that omits what is painful in favor of what is presentable is just another locked door on Weber Street.

The children on that block deserved better adults. All of us did.

In the middle of all this, a different kind of past walked back into my life.

I first met Adrienne when she was thirteen and I was fifteen. We were kids in Kitchener then: awkward, hopeful, moving through high school hallways with that mixture of bravado and confusion that comes with having no idea who you're going to be yet.

We had been on exactly one date when we were teenagers. She was fourteen, I was fifteen. Her mother had made me come to her office to ask permission. Nancy, perhaps charmed by my persistence, granted her blessing. The date itself was a disaster. We sat through *The River*, a Sissy Spacek and Mel Gibson box office flop, in near-total silence. Adrienne, perhaps too shy or simply uninterested, said almost nothing. There was no second date. We drifted into separate lives and stayed there for more than a decade.

Years later, after my marriage to Jelena had collapsed and my new life consisted of Greyhound commutes, partnership work, Candace's weekends, and a house full of old patterns and asbestos, Adrienne and I crossed paths again. I had been seeing Adrienne at Liberal fundraisers for years before we reconnected, events for Andrew Telegdi, my friend who had climbed from University of Waterloo Student Council president to MP for Waterloo. Each time we crossed paths at the Waterloo Motor Inn or Bingaman Place in Kitchener, she lit up when she saw me. Her mother, Nancy, would beam with pride about my accomplishments, as if the awkward teenager who had once asked permission to date her daughter had somehow vindicated her early assessment.

By then, Adrienne was an itinerant neonatal intensive care nurse at The Hospital for Sick Children in Toronto, one of the most prestigious employers in her field. She ended her marriage to an actuary who had lived in Oakville. I was a lawyer at Borden & Elliot, recently divorced from Jelena, commuting between Toronto and Kitchener, living with my mother at 136 Young Street.

On January 17, 2003, my phone rang. A woman's voice asked, "Do you remember me?"

I did. We met for dinner at East Side Mario's near the University of Waterloo. This time, there was no silence. We talked easily, laughed at the same things, and found rhythms that had been missing in 1986. After dinner, we stopped at a convenience store and bought candy—she loved candy—and drove back to 136 Young Street. In the living room of the house I shared with my mother, I kissed her.

Years later, she would recall that moment fondly, remembering the smell of the spearmint leaves I had been eating since childhood, the sweetness that lingered on my breath.

Our relationship moved fast. Too fast for my mother's liking, though that would become clear only later. What I remember most from those early months is the kindness. I had never been treated with such consistent, uncomplicated love. Adrienne woke before 5:00 a.m., drove out of her way to pick me up at Young Street, then backtracked so I could grab coffee at Tim Hortons before she dropped me at the Greyhound station. She would kiss me goodbye, watch me board the bus, and drive back to her day. After work, she would pick me up again. We would have dinner at Northern Thai, our favorite restaurant up the block from the station—crispy beef and pad thai, the same order every time.

I had never felt so much love.

I was sure I wanted to marry her. I was equally sure that if I told her the truth about my life, the mounting debt, the bankruptcy looming on the horizon, the bitter custody battle with Jelena, the wreckage of my first marriage, she would leave. So, I kept it secret for five months.

In May 2003, over dinner at Northern Thai, I finally told her everything. The financial collapse, the fight over Candace, the court dates, the shame. I braced for her to stand up and walk out. Instead, she reached across the table and said, “Don’t worry. We’ll make it through these hardships together.”

Then she added, “But first, we have to sell the house.”

From that moment, I knew I could not let this woman go, even if it meant that the two closest women in my life would eventually grow to hate each other.

Financially, the arithmetic at Young Street was unforgiving. The mortgage, support obligations, commuting costs, and general expense of trying to rebuild a life after divorce pressed hard against my income. The house that was supposed to be a symbol of stability became another source of strain.

Ultimately, something had to give. The thing that could give was the house. Selling 136 Young meant more than letting go of stone and stucco. It meant uprooting my mother again, this time from a place she had just begun to trust. For her, the move to Young Street had been a rescue, so the sale felt like betrayal. For me, it was triage. For both of us, it reopened wounds we had never really closed.

We argued. Old phrases from Weber made their way into a new kitchen. My decision to sell confirmed, for her, that I could not be relied upon. Her response confirmed, for me, that no amount of effort would ever fully repair the past. We did not resolve it. We moved on because the bank and the calendar left us no choice.

Adrienne and I compressed our lives into a smaller space. We rented a unit on Poplar Plains Road in Toronto, a bright but slightly melancholic 1970s apartment building squeezed between expensive homes in lower Forest Hill, just south of St. Clair.

It had no balconies. Apartment 606 was clean, well furnished, and almost comically small, roughly the size of my first apartment on the twenty-ninth floor of 40 Gerrard Street East. But this time, there were no cockroaches. That alone felt like proof that something in my trajectory had improved. I was also much closer to work at what was now called Borden Lander Gervais, LLP. Adrienne could work from home, but travelled often, auditing clinical trials in medical offices.

We adopted a tiny white and scruffy Shih-Poo and named him Joey. The building did not allow dogs, so we smuggled him in and out under our coats, hearts hammering in the elevator whenever it stopped on another floor. It was a small rebellion, an act of shared mischief that seemed harmless compared to everything else we were juggling. We laughed at our own cunning.

Poplar Plains had its own texture: the sound of the streetcar on St. Clair drifting up through the windows; neighbors complaining quietly in the laundry room; the view of other people's larger houses from our living room window. In that modest space, Adrienne and I began to understand what it meant to be together without the cloak of Bay Street status or a detached, three-bedroom corner house to hide in. It was a new hopeful beginning for both of us.

The subway ride to the Scotia Plaza took twenty minutes and the walk to the Ontario Bar Association (OBA) headquarters on Toronto Street was only five minutes further east. This proximity reignited some of my not-for-profit ambitions and helped me rise through the ranks of the OBA until I landed on its Executive Committee. It was a singular honor that I wore with pride, but not joy. That emotion had been, by the age of thirty-five, permanently extinguished. Soon enough, I would think to myself, even the leadership of the OBA would realize they had made a mistake.

In July 2004, Adrienne and I traded small and central for bigger and farther west. We moved into a five-bedroom rental house in Mississauga, forty-five minutes down the Queen Elizabeth Way from downtown Toronto. The house stood on a quiet cul-de-sac. It was large and in a poor state of repair, with a deferred kind of maintenance that shows up as peeling paint, older fixtures, and a general sense that everything works but nothing quite matches. The last tenants loved ladybugs. There was nowhere to look without stumbling across some version of the motif. Even the grand oak tree out front seemed embarrassed to have to wear a large, plastic ladybug screwed harshly to its bark. *I had seen worse*, I thought to myself. This would do.

The house also had space and a backyard, so for five-year-old Candace, it was a gift. She had her own room. She had a safe street lined with mature trees and kids her age, a cul-de-sac where bikes, street chalk, and skipping ropes ruled the asphalt until dusk. For me, it was a compromise I was willing to make. It had less glamor than Palace Place, more distance from the office, but a kind of domestic normalcy I had never really known. This was the way to be a father. For a while, I dared to think I was happy.

Adrienne and I lived there with Joey and our shared hope that this time, the frame would hold. The house became the backdrop for ordinary things: dinners, arguments, laughter, fatigue. I commuted. I worked and worked out. I tried to be present for Candace when she stayed with us. Adrienne worked on clinical trials, then eventually moved to medical device sales. We did our best learning the rhythms of each other's moods and silences.

On October 9, 2005, we were married at Langdon Hall in Cambridge, Ontario. Langdon Hall is an old estate, all brick and wood and carefully tended grounds, the kind of place where you can almost hear the footsteps of other people's histories in the hallways. We did not fill it with relatives. By then, my relationship with my family was badly frayed.

My brothers and I were not on speaking terms. My decision to sell the Young street house had driven a wedge between us and our relationship never recovered. To them, the sale looked like abandoning our mother and erasing one more piece of our parents' story. To me, it had been an act of financial survival that came at a personal cost I hadn't fully understood. To my mother, it was a betrayal, orchestrated by Adrienne, that she would never forgive.

My mother did not attend the wedding, but I didn't invite her. By then, things between her and Adrienne were so strained that Adrienne refused my family's presence. Her logic was sound. I was getting married in secret, in a place where many people orchestrate public celebrations.

Candace was the flower girl, walking carefully down the aisle with small, deliberate steps, grasping the bouquet as if her life depended on it. My friend, Chip, the same friend who had once lent me his grandmother's urine-scented recliner for my apartment on Gerrard Street East, stood beside me as my best man. It was a small gathering, intimate by necessity and by design.

We exchanged vows in a quiet room, under a glass ceiling. There were no elaborate light displays, no large crowd waiting for a kiss to cheer. There was, instead, the weight of two people in their thirties who had already lived through failed marriages and financial strain, daring to say out loud that they believed they could do better this time.

For our honeymoon, we did not fly anywhere. Adrienne and I canoed for two hours down the Grand River; the banks lined with spectacular foliage falling in red and gold. The air was crisp. The water carried us past trees that had seen generations of people float and fish and think their own thoughts. It was simple and quiet and affordable.

I promised her that when our finances were more stable, I would take her on a "real" honeymoon. She accepted that promise in good faith, and I meant it when I made it. The numbers on my spreadsheets had a different opinion. Like our vows, it was a promise that couldn't be kept.

We returned to Mississauga and to the large, tired house that held our optimism and our unresolved problems. Candace ran through its rooms. Joey slept at our feet. From a distance, it looked like a second palace: not made of glass and marble this time, but of brick and hope.

Chapter 24

The Insolvent Success

> *I don't deserve to be happy. I don't deserve what I have or what I want. I don't deserve to be loved or admired.*
>
> —Journal entry, January 2, 2007, age 38

THE SECOND PALACE began to buckle under arithmetic.

By the end of 2005, the financial pressure that had been humming in the background for years became impossible to ignore. Divorce, child support, the costs of maintaining more than one household, years of accumulated debt, and the rent at our Mississauga house all converged. I was a successful trial lawyer with a partner's résumé and a bill collector's mail stack.

From the outside, I looked stable enough. I wore the suit, argued the motions, shook the hands. Inside, the numbers were exact and merciless.

I had developed a habit of stacking certain envelopes on the kitchen counter instead of opening them. Bank statements, credit card bills, overdue notices. Anything that might confirm what I already suspected that I was spending more than I was earning, went into a quiet pile that grew until it became a structure, a paper monument to avoidance.

Amid this, an opportunity appeared that seemed to answer a question I hadn't quite asked out loud. The Ministry of the Attorney General needed a team lead for its corporate-commercial group. It was a leadership role in government leading trials in cases that involved contracts, construction, and tobacco. The work promised complexity and impact, but of a different kind than Bay Street's. Instead of litigating for corporations and institutions, I could advise the Crown itself. Unfortunately, the salary was substantially lower than what I earned as a partner at BLG. Adrienne accepted this financial hit because she thought it would make me happy. She didn't know it at the time, but the realization was dawning on me that nothing ever would. After trying more than forty medications over eleven years, nothing relieved, for any meaningful time, my profound sense of self-loathing and worthlessness. The depressive pain was immense, intolerable, and irremediable.

On December 12, 2005, I left private practice and walked into 720 Bay Street as a civil servant. I told people I was trading income for meaning, that I wanted to be closer to the center of how decisions were made. That was true. It was also true that I was exhausted by the demands and culture of Bay Street and could not see myself sprinting at that pace until retirement.

The Ministry of the Attorney General was a different universe. There were no clients to entertain, no billable targets to report, no need to chase business. There were, instead, briefing notes, cabinet submissions, inter-ministerial committees. The law felt closer to its legislative source, less like a product and more like infrastructure.

My treatment-resistant depression came with me. So did every unpaid bill. The pay cut, layered over existing obligations, reduced the margin between what came in and what went out to the width of a razor blade. The landlord still expected rent. Utilities still expected payment. Groceries still had to be bought. Support payments did not shrink because I had adopted a more altruistic job description.

Within weeks, it was clear that I could not outrun the math. I found myself in a trustee's office, explaining how a man with a law degree, a partnership history, and a new government title had fallen this far behind. The trustee was professional and kind in the way people become when they spend their careers helping others admit defeat. He explained the mechanics of a consumer proposal: list your debts, offer to pay back a portion over time, give creditors more than they would receive in a bankruptcy, and hope they accept.

On January 29, 2006, with his help, I filed a consumer proposal. The document was clinical. It reduced years of effort, miscalculation, and bad luck to columns and totals. I signed it at the same kitchen table where I had tried to build a second marriage, my signature neat and practiced, my stomach in knots.

Creditors are rarely impressed by human context. They considered the offer and indicated, in various ways, that they wanted more. We revised the proposal, increased the payments, tightened an already suffocating budget. We revised it again. Each revision required another admission: I had less room to maneuver than I had pretended.

On March 6, 2006, the creditors voted and rejected the amended proposal. Among the creditors who voted against the proposal was my mother. She had lent me money to help forestall what I refused to believe was inevitable. Drawn from a portion of her equity in 282 Weber, by someone who had never enjoyed the financial cushions my career promised. I could not repay her. I betrayed her again. My rain knew no limits. I knew no shame. On the creditor list, she was not "Mom"; she was a name and a dollar amount. Her vote carried the same weight as that of any bank. It was one more proof that, whatever I thought I had rescued her from by dragging her out of Weber, I had not rescued us from each other, and she was worse off for having trusted me.

The only option was bankruptcy. The trustee explained the consequences. My assets, such as they were, would be gathered for the benefit of my creditors. I would live under a different set of constraints for nine months when, if I complied with the regime, the Court would automatically discharge all of my debts and give me a second chance to rebuild. The bankruptcy was mine alone. Adrienne was not implicated, not directly at least.

The legal declaration of bankruptcy did not arrive in isolation. The same day the proposal failed, and the bankruptcy took effect, a flatbed truck came for my car.

In January 2001, when I was invited into the partnership at what was now Borden Ladner Gervais (BLG), I had celebrated by buying a Porsche Boxster. It was the kind of car a boy from Weber Street never expects to drive, low and impractical and entirely unnecessary. During the worst moments of my divorce from Jelena, driving that car with the roof down had been a small reprieve, a reminder that some part of my life belonged to a world beyond custody timetables and litigation. Now it was collateral.

I watched through the front window as men in work boots hooked the Boxster to a winch. The front end tilted, then the back wheels lifted off the driveway entirely. For a moment it hung there, absurd and helpless, before the truck pulled away. The car that had once felt like a triumph was heading out to be sold at auction for the benefit of the people I owed, including my mother.

Bankruptcy did not stop anything else. In February 2006, Jelena returned to family court in Windsor, seeking to alter the terms of our settlement. She wanted more support and changes to my access to Candace.

From her perspective, my financial implosion made me less reliable. From mine, it made me more desperate to hold on to whatever relationship with my daughter the court would allow.

Adrienne and I drove her car the five hours along the 401, affidavits and binders in the back seat. We stayed up late at the dining room table, sorting documents, rehearsing cross-examinations like lines in a play. When we arrived at the Windsor courthouse on December 11, 2006, there was no performance. After a flurry of negotiation in the corridors, we settled. The agreement preserved enough access that I felt I could live with it. It set new support obligations that, while heavy, seemed less catastrophic than the uncertainties of a trial.

Adrienne was furious. We drove home in a near-unbroken silence. The anger didn't flare and burn out; it cooled into something hard-edged, an irritation that lurked behind many conversations. I could not bring her around to my view of the settlement. She could not convince me that I had betrayed us. The matter hung unresolved between us, like so much else.

Chapter 25

The Candidate's Floor

> *The thought of suicide is a great consolation: by means of it one gets through many a dark night.*
>
> — Friedrich Nietzsche, *Beyond Good and Evil*

IN JUNE OF 2007, the Ontario Bar Association, the largest volunteer association of lawyers in the province, serving 16,000 members, elected me Treasurer. The irony was thick enough to spread with a knife: the new Treasurer of the OBA was, unknown to them, a recently discharged bankrupt. I chaired meetings about budgets and governance and the financial health of the association while my own economic history had supervised by a trustee. While the profession saw me as a safe pair of hands for its money, my creditors had disagreed. My mother had disagreed.

At the age of thirty-nine, my life had split into two parallel tracks. On one track, I was a senior lawyer at the Ministry of the Attorney General for Ontario, part of a team trying to manage the Caledonia land dispute without spilling blood, and Treasurer of the OBA, sitting at boardroom tables talking about governance and policy, chairing meetings, shaking hands. On the other track, I was a man in a rented house in Mississauga, bankrupt, in a second marriage that was already fraying, spending long stretches in a dark spare room wishing I could disappear.

Most evenings followed the same choreography. I would come home from 720 Bay and, instead of walking into the kitchen or living room, head straight upstairs to the spare room. I would close the door, draw the curtains, and lie on the bed for hours. No television, no music, no light. Just the hum of the house and the louder hum of my own thoughts. *You are exhausting everyone around you. You are too much. Everyone would be better off if you were gone.*

It felt less like self-pity than bookkeeping: reviewing the debits and credits and realizing the ledger did not balance.

Adrienne knocked during these retreats. She would sit on the edge of the bed, ask what was wrong, try to coax me out. Over time, the knocks grew less frequent. There are only so many times a person can be turned away or met with silence before they begin to protect themselves. She had married the version of me who could chair meetings and make jokes at dinner, not the man who vanished upstairs for hours at a time. At first, she treated my retreats like a problem to solve. Over time, they became the rugged terrain she was forced to navigate every day.

Her frustration eventually found clear, sharp language. "If you're depressed," she said one evening, "it's because you want to be."

The words landed like a judgment. I didn't get angry. I agreed with her. If even the person closest to me saw my sadness as a choice, then maybe it was. Maybe I was choosing this. Maybe this really was my fault. It was a harsh sentence to say out loud, but didn't feel cruel—rather more like despair reduced to words. She had watched me vanish and return and vanish again for years. If she could convince herself I was choosing this, then she could also believe I might choose differently. But I had to ask myself why anyone would choose this. If I had a choice, and made it against all reason, despite the shadows it cast about, how could I hope or ask or deserve help? The shame of my condition, and the possibility that it could be self-inflicted, compelled me to try harder to hide it, even as my self-worth spiralled into caverns deeper than death.

At the Ministry of the Attorney General, the Caledonia file crowded out everything else. Douglas Creek Estates, a new subdivision in Caledonia, had been occupied by Six Nations land defenders who maintained that it sat on unceded land. Tensions escalated quickly. There were blockades of Highway 6 and a nearby CN rail line. Tires burned. Confrontations between residents, police, and protesters grew in intensity. Everyone carried the memory of Ipperwash.

In 1995, an unarmed Ojibwe man named Dudley George had been shot and killed by an Ontario Provincial Police officer during a protest at Ipperwash Provincial Park. The inquiry that followed laid bare a pattern of political interference, racism, and failure. Its thousands of pages sat in the background of every conversation about Caledonia like a warning siren.

Before key court appearances, the instruction to our litigation team was blunt: try not to get anyone killed. We were reminded that the words we used in a courtroom in Cayuga—the positions we took on injunctions and enforcement, the tone we adopted in front of a judge—could either cool or inflame a situation on the ground where people with real weapons and older grievances stood face to face. It was a sobering reminder that law is not an abstract exercise. It can get people hurt.

So, the days filled with balancing acts: how to assert the authority of the courts without repeating past violence; how to acknowledge Indigenous land rights in a framework that had so often denied them; how to write submissions that signalled firmness without contempt.

The work consumed me in the hours I could stand upright. It also gave me cover. If the crisis in Caledonia needed my full attention, I did not have to look too closely at the crisis in my own head.

Bankruptcy, meanwhile, hummed along in the background like a broken appliance. It was not just a legal status; it was a constant whisper in every decision: Can we afford this? What happens if something breaks?

The titles accumulated. So did the weight behind my eyes.

> *I am going to be nominated as the Liberal candidate for Kitchener–Conestoga! ...*
>
> *Where am I going to find the confidence to do this?*
>
> —Journal entry, November 19, 2007, age 39

AROUND THAT TIME, an accident shook the political world in Waterloo Region. A former federal Liberal Member of Parliament had been badly injured in a crash. The rumors that followed were not public, but they travelled quickly: that it might have been a suicide attempt. No one confirmed them. No one had to. They floated in the air like a cautionary tale, an unspoken reminder that even highly admired people in high office could be quietly unravelling.

The party needed a new candidate in Kitchener–Conestoga, which was familiar ground: Kitchener, surrounding townships, smaller communities filled with people whose stories looked a lot like my parents' and my own. Factories, farms, small businesses, immigrant families who had arrived with nothing and built something out of it. People who still believed, some days more than others, that politics could make their lives better. It also contained a significant Portuguese community that formed in the 1960s from immigrants leaving the same region of northern Portugal that gave life to my father and nurtured my paternal great-grandfather, while later participating in the pretense that disguised his suicide as something more respectable—a murder. This, in turn, allowed him a Catholic burial in the cemetery I visited with my father in 1979 in Oporto.

Although suicidal ideation dominated my thoughts after-hours, I put forward my name for the Liberal nomination, seemingly continuing the incongruent and growing divide between my personal and professional life: the bankrupt OBA Treasurer; the suicidal candidate daring to replace another possibly suicidal candidate; the successful man resigning himself to believe he could only ever fail, still trying to win. My reasons were layered and not entirely noble. Part of me believed, still, that public office was a way to make meaning, to shape laws and policies so that fewer people would fall through the cracks that had nearly swallowed me. Part of me wanted a new frame: something large and outward facing, with signs and slogans, to eclipse the inner narrative that I was a ruined man taking others down with him. Part of me quietly hoped that if I became a federal candidate, Adrienne might see me differently. That if I was chosen by a riding, I might be chosen, again, by her.

Pursuing the nomination meant adding another job to days that were already supercharged. I spent eight or nine hours at 720 Bay, working on Ministry files, then got into the car and drove about two hours west along Highway 401 to Kitchener, where I went door to door in the Portuguese community, selling Liberal memberships.

As expected, many of the people I visited had come from the same Minho region of Portugal as my father. Arriving in Canada in the 1960s and 1970s, they took jobs in factories, on construction sites, in bakeries, and bought modest houses with vegetable gardens and leafy backyard patios. They remembered my father. And they remembered my mother. Some remembered me as a boy, but not for reasons I would have hoped. Some told me how, on Samuel Street, my mother had the notorious habit of leaving me outside unattended for, what must have seemed like hours, strapped in a stroller during bright cold winter days. I don't remember this, but it was whispered to me as if disclosing a scandalous truth. Much later, during a funeral wake for my uncle, several members of the Portuguese community reintroduced themselves to my mother and reminded her of this long-abandoned habit. She felt flattered to be remembered and confirmed that she hadn't neglected me, she simply needed her rest and her smokes. I was never that far from view. She didn't mention the cold; nor why anyone would remember this more than fifty years later.

During the summer of 2007, I stood on the porches in the fading light and told the Portuguese community why I wanted to represent them in Ottawa. I spoke about being the child of immigrants, about law and fairness, about wanting to make sure the next generation had more stability than my parents. I asked them to buy a ten-dollar membership and show up to vote for me at the nomination meeting.

They asked about jobs and pensions, about their children's prospects, about whether anyone in Ottawa ever really listened. They also asked after my family: How is your mom? Your brothers? Are you okay, Orlando?

The questions blurred politics and family until I could not tell where one ended and the other began. On those porches, I was not just a candidate; I was a boy from Weber Street reporting back to an extended village about what he had done with his life.

Sometimes they hugged me at the door. Sometimes they pressed the membership fee into my hand with a kind of proud defiance, as if they were buying stock in a distant cousin. I would leave their houses with my clipboard a little heavier and my chest a little lighter, then drive east in the dark and feel the light go out again before I reached Mississauga.

The nomination meeting took place on 24 November 2007, in a rented hall, folding chairs lined in rows, the air thick with coffee, perfume, and anticipation. The room was full of faces I knew, old family friends, community leaders, lawyers, activists, people who had knocked on doors for other candidates long before anyone knew my name.

My speech was a compressed version of my life story: immigrant family, Weber Street, the student leader awards, law school, Bay Street, Caledonia. I told them I knew what it was to feel disposable and what it was to be given a second chance. I promised that if they chose me, I would fight for people who didn't have the time or the language or the money to fight for themselves. I did not breathe a word about depression, anxiety, or mental health.

They applauded at the right moments. They laughed at the lighter lines. Since the inevitable results had become clear weeks earlier, the riding president announced my victory as the room rose to its feet. It should have been a moment of uncomplicated joy: bullied, slow, rain cloud from Weber Street, not the federal Liberal candidate in a riding imprinted on his childhood. But I had lost the capacity for joy many years earlier.

Part of me was grateful. Part of me was numb. Underneath both was the familiar voice that said: if they knew the truth, they would never have chosen you. Leave before they discover the decaying voids you're hiding. Because while everyone saw a victory, I saw an adjournment in a trial I was prosecuting against myself.

A year earlier, Adrienne had already begun to withdraw. For months, the house, once a hopeful symbol of a new stability, became the unforgiving and hollowed memorial to yet another failed marriage.

One night, Adrienne left. There was no single dramatic scene, no slammed door that echoed down the years. She had tried everything she knew how to try: conversations, invitations, ultimatums, silence. It wasn't that she had stopped caring; it was that caring no longer seemed to make a difference. Her clothes, her books, her presence in the rooms receded until the house was mostly just me, some furniture, and the hum of appliances I couldn't fix.

On December 27, 2007, I packed my life into boxes again and moved back to Kitchener, into a bleak student apartment on Old Carriage Drive. My fifth-floor unit overlooked a parking lot, Highway 8, and a row of overflowing dumpsters. When the windows were open, the smell of rotting vegetables and the noise of a thousand cars assaulted me.

The kitchen floor was cheap linoleum, its pattern worn to a dull gray smudge in front of the sink and stove. The overhead light was a harsh fluorescent tube that buzzed faintly and cast everything in a sickly, jaundiced glow. But it would cost me $810 a month, and it was within the riding. It would have to do, for now.

From there, my commute to work became a two-hour Greyhound trip each way, a four-hour daily purgatory between identities. Late at night, I would get off near Old Carriage Drive, walk back through the parking lot, unlock the door, and scornfully meet the hum of the fridge and the rectangular pool of jaundiced light from the kitchen. I tried not to think of the days when Candace, still a baby, greeted me joyfully at the door of Palace Place.

The campaign unfolded from Old Carriage Drive. Weekends and evenings were a blur of lawn signs, debates, and doorsteps. I shook hands at fall fairs and church picnics. Campaign days started early and ended late. Some mornings I would catch the Greyhound at dawn, work a full day in Toronto, return to Kitchener in the early evening, and go straight from the bus stop to door knocking. We would finish a canvass, debrief in someone's living room or around a kitchen table, and then I would walk back to my own kitchen, where there was no one to debrief with at all. Like all my private torments, no one knew Adrienne had left.

On the way to events, alone in the car or on the bus, I would rehearse two parallel futures. In one, I won and became a Member of Parliament. I commuted to Ottawa, sat on committees, and spoke in the House. I kept my depression hidden and hoped that public visibility would frighten it into retreat.

In the other, I lost. I went back to 720 Bay and to Old Carriage Drive with nothing but the debt, the strain, and the confirmation that even when hundreds of people heard my story, it wasn't enough.

Both futures shared a common feature: I did not know how to imagine myself as simply alive and ordinary, not failing and not performing. The middle ground remained inaccessible.

Election night arrived in the usual colors: red for us, blue for them, numbers crawling along the bottom of television screens. We gathered in a pub in Kitchener, the walls draped in banners, supporters clutching plastic cups and hope.

As results trickled in, it became clear that the national narrative was not going our way. In Kitchener–Conestoga, in under twenty minutes, my Conservative opponent was declared the winner. My total was large enough to look respectable and small enough to be decisive. I came second, with no silver medal.

> *Well...I lost by almost 12,000 votes. It wasn't even close. I don't know how to fill the void.*
>
> —Journal entry, October 16, 2008, age 40

I walked up to each volunteer who had spent evenings and weekends knocking on doors, elders from the Portuguese community who had believed I could carry their stories to Ottawa, friends who had driven in from Toronto. They looked tired, worried, and still, somehow, proud.

I thanked them. I congratulated my opponent. I said the mandatory lines about democracy and service and the privilege of running. My voice was steady. My heart was not.

At St. Jerome's High School, our Principal, Father Mike Cundari, taught us to "win with dignity and lose with pride." Taking that sentiment to heart, I decided I would drive, alone, to my opponent's celebration party to congratulate him personally. When I arrived, his supporters applauded as one of my old high school football coaches gave me a bear hug that I can still feel today. He didn't vote for me, but he was still on my side. It was, in its own way, a kind of success: I had lost well.

Throughout the riding, volunteers quickly removed my signs from the lawns of my supporters, closed the campaign office, and then dispersed. Back at Old Carriage Drive, my phone rang less and then not at all. The riding moved on to whatever came after disappointment.

Inside the apartment, my narrative hardened.

You have failed as a husband twice. You are a financial burden.

Your daughter is better off without your chaos.

You are taking up space someone better could use.

The student apartment on Old Carriage Drive was supposed to be temporary, a way to be closer to the people and places that had made me. Instead, it became the narrow corridor between my public life and the intolerable pain that I was hiding, that I had always hid. It was on the kitchen floor of that Old Carriage Drive apartment, beneath the buzzing fluorescent light, that I came as close as a person can to dying. What happened next, what I did to myself, what was found, how I woke up under hospital lights, amounts to the methodical narrowing of a life left to the cold linoleum in the kitchen of a student apartment, two hours by bus from Bay Street.

The former candidate, the Crown counsel, the Treasurer of the OBA—all those roles were still technically mine. But by the time my body hit the kitchen floor, I was no longer living as any of them. I was a simply a man convinced that dying would be my last and greatest act of love.

Chapter 26

The Ward

> *I am concerned for my survival.*
>
> —Journal entry, February 22, 2009, age 40

ALTHOUGH I HAVE nothing but fragmented memories of my suicide attempt, the memories I recovered and assembled over the weeks and months that followed represents my best attempt at a coherent retelling. The first thing I remember after the kitchen floor was light being forced into my eyes. The cold of the vinyl was gone, replaced by the bite of straps and the sway of motion. A high, distant wail of a siren filtered into my awareness.

Someone was saying my name. Someone else was telling me to stay with them. The siren was an underwater sound, but what cut through more clearly was the click and scrape of glass, empty bottles clanking together somewhere behind my head as the ambulance bounced over winter streets.

"Vodka... wine... beer..." a voice muttered, reading labels as if they were evidence. Another voice read the names on the prescription vials they'd gathered from my counter, my bedside table, the bathroom.

"Sertraline. Wellbutrin. Seroquel. Clonazepam. Temazepam. Ativan. Zopiclone. Zyprexa. Lamictal. Trazadone. Effexor. Venlafaxine. Mirtazapine. Citalopram." A flashlight bored into my pupils again. "Orlando, look at me!"

I tried to close my eyes against the narrow violence of the beam. The paramedic followed, steady, relentless, like cross-examination. I was strapped down. I could feel the movement of the stretcher, the sway of the vehicle, but my body might as well have belonged to someone else. The straps bit into my chest and legs every time the ambulance turned.

The siren grew louder as we approached the hospital and then cut off suddenly, leaving a whine of silence in my ears. We stopped and the doors swung open. Cold air came in, biting and metallic. "Let's go," someone said, and then I was moving again, pulled out, jostled, the stretcher legs snapping down, my body lifted and rolled forward into fluorescent light.

I caught glimpses of automatic doors, a ceiling grid, faces hanging over me like masks. The bottles clanked again. Somewhere behind my head, something rattled with each uneven patch of pavement.

I slipped in and out of consciousness as doctors and nurses worked around me with focused intensity. I was barely aware of their presence, let alone what they were doing, or why. Once the medical emergency had been overcome, during what could have been hours or days, for all I knew, a psychiatrist stood at beside my bed with Adrienne at her side.

Shortly after our conversation, I was wheeled toward a locked set of doors. Two security guards stood on either side, arms folded, eyes scanning the traffic in and out. When they saw my face, they straightened.

"Hey, Orlando," one of them said, surprised. "We saw you on the signs during the campaign." He said it the way you might greet a neighbor at the grocery store.

It took me a moment to understand that I still had a public existence outside this stretcher. The memory of my name, my face, my red signs lingered, even as I was being rolled past the guards into a world where none of that mattered.

The doors buzzed. Someone pressed a button. The locks released with a mechanical clack. As the stretcher moved forward, the doors shut behind us with a soft but final note. The sound of them closing behind me landed like a verdict.

The psychiatric ward was crowded. It was mid-December 2008. Outside, the streets were freezing. Inside, the air was thick with antiseptic, sweat, institutional food, homelessness, addiction, and fatigue. There were people everywhere, slumped in chairs, standing in doorways, pacing the hallway in slow, heavy circuits.

Many were homeless. You could see it in the layers of clothing, in the way some clutched plastic bags or backpacks as if they contained everything they owned, in the urgency with which they pressed their case at the nursing station.

"It's freezing out there," one elderly woman kept saying. "Please keep me one more night."

A teenager, tugging at his torn parka and endlessly scratching his left arm, agreed, "There is nowhere to go. We're gonna freeze."

The constant hum of the ward was punctuated by sudden screams, the sound of someone struggling against restraints or against a reality only they could see.

Being held in hospital against your will is not gentle. It is fluorescent and loud. It strips you of your street clothes and your decisions. It tells you, in words and deeds, that you are not trusted with your own life. You squandered that right.

At some point, my clothes had been taken away. I found myself in a thin hospital gown that gaped open down the back, the fabric cold against my skin. A nurse showed me how to wear two gowns at once—one tied in front; one tied in back—to preserve some semblance of dignity.

"Like this," she said, her hands quick and practiced. She paused and tugged the back hem down an extra inch. "You don't need any more indignity today."

Paper slippers covered my feet. They made a soft, uncertain sound on the linoleum as I shuffled from bed to bathroom and back.

Patients moved around me in slow motion, heavily sedated. Some stared straight ahead, eyes unfocused, lips moving silently. Others muttered to themselves or to invisible companions. A few carried an uneasily contained irritation; they paced with an uneven, restless anger, bracelets flashing as they turned, occasionally exploding in a burst of shouting or a fist against a wall before staff moved in, calm but firm.

I was placed in a room of eight men; a heavy drawn curtain divided the room into two segments of four, creating the illusion of more privacy but doing nothing for the noise. One man, a patient in his twenties with schizophrenia, sat up all night, every night, pretending to drive his bed like a race car. He provided full commentary and sound effects at the top of his lungs: high-revving acceleration, adept gear changes, hard braking, burnouts, and the roaring approval of an imaginary crowd. "Here we go, last lap—listen to that roaring beast—" He slammed an invisible pedal. He mimed the steering wheel. He whooped and cheered for himself. The performance was complete and relentless.

The nursing staff, already stretched thin, practiced a kind of determined ambivalence. They checked on him, checked on us, adjusted medications, and only half-closed doors. They did not stop the race. In that environment, his crisis was not the loudest one. Sleep was impossible unless you were sedated to the same stupor as everyone else.

Within three days, my involuntary hold expired, leaving the possibility of another one being imposed. Instead, I was offered the opportunity to stay because no noticeable improvement, in that environment, could be seen, or even achieved, in three days. Accepting that I had reached a nadir, I decided to approach the treatment plan they offered as my last best chance to recover. I didn't know how long it would take, but I was prepared to stay as long as I could. In my circumstances, that meant I could use as much as six months of short-term medical leave. They would provide my employer with whatever they needed, subject to my right to privacy. They also offered weekend passes, a formality for voluntary in-patients, so that I may continue to parent three out of four weekends per month.

I still told my family nothing, although they knew but pretended not to. I was grateful for that indulgence. My employer knew I was sick, but not from what. I had no visitors and wanted none. When my willpower and loneliness overcame me, I would call Adrienne, but these became short and sharp reminders of what I had lost. My veil of secrecy helped preserve my dignity, but likely impeded my recovery. In effect, I was saving what was left of my career, from the stigma that would otherwise destroy it, to have something to return to, if Grand River Hospital could save me from myself.

The veil of secrecy did not hold. The police were obliged to inform Candace's mother, Jelena, that I had attempted suicide. She immediately hired a lawyer to schedule an emergency hearing in Windsor to annul, indefinitely, my right to see Candace out of fear, but not evidence, that I was an unfit father. It arrived at the nurse's station and required me to appear in Windsor forty-eight hours later to fight for my right to parent Candace. Although I was not afraid to die, I was terrified of losing my little girl, my sunshine. With the force of will only true emergencies can summon, I wrote an affidavit, explaining my circumstances, and reassuring the court that I was doing my best to recover, and that, under no circumstances, did I pose a danger to Candace or anyone else. My psychiatrist agreed and provided a letter of support.

My best friend Chip, despite his deep concern, helped me print and assemble my affidavit into a record the Court would accept, without asking questions. He also helped me find a lawyer to commission the affidavit. When that lawyer, a distant relative of his, started reading my affidavit (an unnecessary intrusion and professional discourtesy), I ripped it from his hands, insulted his competence, and tracked down my former colleague, Katherine, who practiced law in downtown Kitchener. She came to the hospital, asked nothing about why I was in the psychiatric ward, ran through the steps necessary to commission the affidavit and, after wishing me well, quietly left. We never spoke of that day again.

I attended Court on a day pass, ready to argue my case, as I had done for so many others in so many courts across the province. But this time it was for me. And it was for Candace. To me, the stakes had never been higher. Despite my severe treatment resistant depression, the cocktail of medications developed to quell my desire to die, and regular electro-convulsive shock treatments, I was never more prepared to perform competence and persuasion. After two hours of waiting, and a little more than one hour of argument, the Court declined her lawyer's request to exclude my psychiatrist's letter of support and admonished her lawyer for the attempt. It also refused to grant Jelena's motion. I had won.

I returned to the car in silence. As I sat in the passenger seat, a violent, silent tremor ran through me. My shoulders, clenched for days, finally dropped. The air left my lungs; more reflex than breath. I pressed my hands into my eyes, not to wipe away tears, but to suppress them. My body shuddered with each dry sob as I finally let it break my fall.

The hospital ward awaited my return—and so did life. That evening, I told one of the doctors that whatever else this environment was doing, it wasn't doing much to improve my mental health. I said it lightly, the way lawyers complain about conference food, but I meant it. I was not asking for luxury. I was asking for quiet.

Not long after that, they moved me two floors up, to a different ward, one that housed, as someone put it, "the simply suicidal."

The depression and anxiety ward was a different world. It was still fluorescent. It was still loud. It still smelled of antiseptic and boredom. But the atmosphere was less chaotic, less saturated with intoxication and psychosis and the sheer desperation of people trying to get in from the cold. Here, the focus was depression and anxiety, minds that had turned on their owners in slower, quieter ways.

The ward was filled with adults of every age, demographic, and level of education, but we were nearly indistinguishable in our uniforms: double-wrapped hospital gowns and paper slippers, hair flattened by sleep or meds, faces drained of color by too many long nights and too many small white pills.

In that sameness, some of the old hierarchies of my life fell away. There was no corner office here, no OBA head table, no riding association stage. There were just people sitting in plastic chairs, trying to remember why they were still alive.

Group support sessions formed and reformed. We sat in circles and talked, sometimes haltingly, sometimes with a surprising rush of words, about trauma and medication, about what we had tried before and what had failed us.

We compared notes about side effects and combinations: which antidepressant had helped someone out of bed, which dosage had made another patient feel like a stranger in their own skull. We argued gently about whether therapy was useful or useless, whether exercise was an insult or a lifeline. We laughed, sometimes, at the absurdity of being told to "think positive" in a place where half the patients couldn't summon the energy to shower.

Those conversations spilled over into the rest of the day. They continued around meals—trays balanced on plastic tables, utensils chosen carefully so no one could hurt themselves—or in front of the television, where we watched other people's scripted lives unfold while ours were on hold.

I made temporary friends: a teacher, a factory worker, a graduate student, a retiree. We traded stories in low voices during visiting hours we had chosen not to use, because we were too ashamed to invite anyone in. One man would wordlessly save me a chair at group if I was late, sliding it back with his foot, a small act of belonging. We promised to keep in touch after I was discharged in June 2009, but I never saw him again.

Those were my first tentative steps toward recovery. It was the simple, stubborn discovery that other people understood the anguish of depression, could name it, could sit with it without flinching, and did not treat my wish to die as a reasonable plan.

Treatment came in layers. There were more antidepressants: old ones revisited, new ones added, doses adjusted in the hope that some chemical combination would finally unlock a door in my brain.

There were sleeping pills, anti-anxiety medications, charts tracking vitals and moods. And there was ECT.

Thirteen times, I lay on a narrow bed under operating-room lights while a team moved around me with quiet efficiency. Electroconvulsive therapy sounded medieval when I first heard the words, a punishment more than a treatment. It was strangely mundane.

An anesthesiologist inserted an IV. A nurse attached electrodes to my temples. Someone explained the process again in the calm, rehearsed tone of consent forms, even though my admission remained involuntary and my options were limited.

"You'll be asleep," they said. "You won't feel the seizure."

The anesthetic slid into my vein, cool and irresistible. The ceiling blurred. The next thing I knew, I was in recovery, a different ceiling above me, my jaw aching faintly, my muscles sore, my short-term memory punctured like a sieve.

I did not wake up thinking, *Thank God.* I woke up thinking, *What have I consented to this time?* It seemed like a slow controlled erasure of pieces of myself, but, thankfully, not the whole of me.

For six months, the answer on that ward, whatever its flaws, whatever its cruelties, was not a menu. It was one blunt imperative: you will stay alive long enough to see if your mind still says the same thing tomorrow.

If a clinician had met me an hour before I met the kitchen floor of

Old Carriage Drive, they would have seen a competent, articulate man making a sustained, rational case for his own death. I would have met the criteria for MAiD for mental illness, had it been legislated back then: treatment-resistant, grievous and irremediable suffering, longstanding illness. I believed, with courtroom clarity, that my death would be the greatest act of love to those I loved most.

> *It is a far, far greater thing that I do, than I have ever done. It is a far, far greater rest that I go to, than I have ever known.*
>
> — Dickens, *A Tale of Two Cities*

Six months later, my history was the same. My childhood was the same. The illnesses were the same. The only difference was time, safety, and the stubborn refusal of a few professionals to accept my certainty at face value. They doubted that my desire to die was a feature and not just a bug, against all reason I could muster.

Although I did not leave hospital with a new personality, I did leave with a slightly different relationship to my thoughts. I had watched other patients enter and leave the ward with minds that sounded as convinced as mine had and then softened. I had felt my own verdict—you are a burden, you will never get better, everyone is better off without you—lose its status as fact and become, very slightly, a story my illness was telling.

For a while after discharge, that fragile progress was supported by outpatient groups and follow-up programs that extended the ward's scaffolding into ordinary life. We kept meeting. We kept comparing notes on medications, on sleep, on the daily work of staying.

Then budgets tightened. The notice appeared on the ward's community bulletin board, typed and unsigned: Effective end of month, the Tuesday and Thursday outpatient groups will be discontinued due to funding reallocation. The social worker who ran them called me a week later, her voice tight with apology. “There’s just no money,” she said. “I’m so sorry.” The line went quiet for a moment. “Take care of yourself, Orlando.”

One by one, the groups dissolved. The phone calls grew less frequent as people returned to their own emergencies. In the end, I was left alone with self-renewing prescriptions and no scheduled follow-up for the next two years.

I was outside again. The doors no longer locked behind me. But something had shifted in those six months of fluorescent indignity and enforced survival. The candidate, the confident lawyer, the self-assured leader—all those roles would come back, in different forms, in different rooms. For a long time, I would still be convinced that the most loving thing I could do for the people I cared about was to disappear.

The difference was this: having been strapped to a stretcher, having been admitted against my will, having had my mind treated as unreliable even when it sounded reasonable, I now thought, somewhere beneath the noise, that my own verdict condemning my self-worth *may* be wrong.

It would take years to confirm that timid glimmer of hope. But its first faint outline was drawn there, in two gowns and paper slippers, on a ward full of people who had also tried, in their own ways, to leave and were still, for the moment, in the room.

Chapter 27

Simple Gifts

> *One must imagine Sisyphus happy.*
>
> — Albert Camus, *The Myth of Sisyphus*

The spring air of June 2009 felt like a violation. Too bright. Too full. I had tried so hard to leave, and the world had the audacity to be beautiful.

Old Carriage Drive was as I'd left it: a still life of defeat. Dishes, bottles, the scattered evidence of a life coming undone. Yet the light through the dirty window seemed different. I opened the curtains. I cleaned. Not with purpose, but with a quiet, mechanical insistence, as if order outside could impose order within.

With a few weeks left before I had to return to work, small routines began to form. A seven-minute walk to the Tim Hortons at Pioneer Park Plaza. Hours with a book and a coffee, surrounded by the harmless murmur of strangers. Tuesday nights, I savored the roast beef special at the plaza's diner.

Next door, Blockbuster was still open. Candace and I wandered the aisles, debating Belle versus Ariel, her hand in mine. The weight of it—small, warm, trusting—was an anchor.

I was learning the grammar of staying. Not the grand narratives of success, but the quiet syntax of a walk, a meal, a child's choice of movie. The pills on the counter were a daily footnote: *This peace is manufactured. Handle with care.*

Adrienne lived twenty minutes north now. The distance between us was measured in sidewalks.

Her dogs, Joey and Lucy, became part of my routine. They were two white, scruffy Shih-Poos who didn't know about wards or verdicts. They knew squirrels and the weight of a cloth frisbee, or the feel of a KONG filled with peanut butter in their mouths. Their joy was physical, contagious. Walking them was an act of translation: their simple needs pulling me back into a body I had tried to discard.

My life had shrunk to a manageable size. No titles to chase, no pinnacles to scale. My job was now elemental: breathing, medicate, walk the dogs, show up.

With Candace, smallness was not poverty. It was abundance. In Victoria Park, she fed swans with a solemn focus. At Waterloo Park, she sat at a pottery wheel, her small hands slick with mud, her tongue peeking out in concentration. The bowl she made was lopsided, collapsing slightly on one side.

"Look, Daddy," she said, holding it up like a sacrament. It was perfect.

At Fairview Park Mall, she got her ears pierced. She chose tiny studs from a card, sat very straight in the high chair, and didn't flinch when the guns clicked. Afterward, she studied her reflection, tilting her head. "I look older," she declared.

And I, for once, didn't think of all the milestones I might miss. I just stood there, a man who had somehow made it to a mall on a Tuesday and saw my daughter becoming herself.

On a lark, at Adrienne's urging, I bought five dozen eggs and took them to the woods to throw at the trees, one after another. The sound was a wet, satisfying *thwack*. Yolk slid down bark like slow tears. I roared with each throw. Not in anger, but in a kind of wild, purposeless release. For ten minutes, I was not a patient, a case, a problem. I was a man in the woods, laughing at the glorious, stupid waste of it.

The darkness did not leave. It sat in the passenger seat, a familiar companion. But it was no longer driving.

By July, the practical world resumed its claim. My unused office chair in Toronto would be gathering dust. Files waited. So, I packed my briefcase, its weight both familiar and foreign.

At the bus stop, I boarded the Greyhound. Same route. Same rattling heater. Same blue seats smelling of old fabric and other lives. But I was not the same man commuting between performances. I was a man returning from a long exile, carrying a fragile, hard-won truth: the most profound act of defiance is not a grand gesture, but the decision to reenter an ordinary day.

The frame of my life had cracked. But as the highway unspooled toward the city, I realized I no longer wanted to escape the picture. I wanted to step back inside and see what might happen next.

Chapter 28

A Fresh Ambition

> *I had a pretty good day today. I slept last night (thank God) and had lunch with a colleague. We spent an hour or so talking about a file. I felt "substantial and intelligent".*
>
> —Journal entry, April 13, 2011, age 42

For a few months after the ward, I kept commuting from Kitchener. The Greyhound remained a corridor between identities. But as strength and savings allowed, I moved again, this time back to Toronto, to an apartment at 40 Gerrard Street West.

It stood where Bay Street intersected Gerrard. Law and hospital, money and medicine, crossing at street level. My commute shrank to a five-minute walk, delayed only by a red light at the corner.

My days began to follow a new, manageable pattern. Walk to work at 720 Bay for the Ministry of the Attorney General. Try to do one useful thing. Walk home. Eat something simple. Sleep or at least try to. My files were returned to me, with some modest steps taken to advance them toward trial. I did not explain my long absence, though colleagues likely deduced some measure of the truth.

In the evenings, when the old urge to disappear tugged at me, I turned to something I had started in 1986, the year I helped create OSAID. My journal.

It was battered by then and had spilled into several volumes, a line of spines stretching back across decades. I had never been a daily diarist. I only wrote in it when I was depressed or anxious, when the weather in my head turned dangerous.

Reading it at the small table on Gerrard Street, I noticed something I had never been able to see from inside the storms. The long blanks. Entries written in a tight, desperate hand would run for pages: *I will never feel better; I always ruin everything; I can't remember not feeling this way.*

Then: nothing. Weeks, sometimes months, of white space. Then, again, another cluster of dark entries declaring that I had always been like this and always would be.

The blank spaces contradicted my certainty. They were quiet witnesses of times when I had put the journal down and gone back to living. Times when I had been well enough that I didn't need to write at all. Depression told me it was permanent, immovable. The chronology on the page said otherwise. It was cyclical.

That realization gave me something I hadn't had on the kitchen floor: evidence against my own mind. When I was depressed, I could never remember not being depressed. I believed I would never recover. But the journal said I always had, even if only temporarily. If that pattern held, then the dark I was in at any given moment might not be an endless tunnel. It might be another bend.

On a day when the light felt strong enough, I wrote myself a letter. I addressed it to the version of me that lay on floors and hospital beds, the one who believed he was doing everyone a favor by leaving. I explained, as calmly as I could, that he was not to be trusted. That his mind was sick. That every previous time he had felt this certain about his worthlessness, he had later been proven wrong.

I told him to read the journal, to look at the blank spaces. I asked him to wait out the darkness—day by day, hour by hour, sometimes one breath at a time—until he could see even the faintest outline of another possibility. I folded the letter and slipped it into the journal. It was not a cure. It was a note in a bottle, addressed to a future self I hoped would still be reachable.

Around that time, I began to reinhabit other parts of myself I had abandoned. I returned to reading the kinds of books that had first made the world feel larger than Weber Street: Ken Follett's epics, Greg Iles's thrillers, Conn Iggulden's historical sagas. Their characters carried burdens that weren't mine for a few hours at a stretch. Battles were fought, cities besieged, empires rose and fell. Compared to those arcs, my own disasters felt, if not small, at least survivable.

Partly out of nostalgia and partly to pay homage to my father, I resumed violin lessons. I had quit when I was sixteen, days after he moved to Toronto to work at McDonnell Douglas, leaving my mother, brothers, and me to our own quiet war in Kitchener. Now, decades later, I stood in a small practice room with the instrument under my chin, fingers stiff, bowing out scales that squeaked and scratched.

My teacher was patient. "You're starting again," he said. "Not starting from nothing." The distinction lodged somewhere deep. It applied to more than music.

I walked everywhere, rediscovering downtown Toronto on foot, often with Candace in tow. We wandered the brick lanes of the Distillery District, the air smelling of coffee and old stone. We cut through the quiet squares and oldest buildings at the University of Toronto's St. George campus, where the ivy seemed older than my career.

We sat in the cafeteria at the Royal Conservatory of Music, listening to students argue about auditions and composers. At Hart House Theatre, Candace and I watched *Macbeth* from worn seats, the actors' voices echoing off the high ceiling. She leaned forward, eyes wide, mouthing lines she had only just heard. Something in that dark Scottish tragedy lit a fuse in her. It would grow into a lifelong love of theater and literature. I watched her watching the stage and felt, for once, not like a man failing at fatherhood, but like one quietly passing on a torch, a torch my own father once tried to hide in his closet.

My curiosity, long diverted into law and policy, found other outlets. I enrolled in a Renaissance history course at York University, partly to satisfy my love of that period, partly to complete the pieces of my unfinished degree from Waterloo. A few nights a week, I sat in a classroom with students half my age, taking notes on Medici politics and Florentine banking, my brain stretching around something other than written arguments and defenses.

On the days when even that felt like too much, I let my attention narrow to the screen. I immersed myself in endless episodes of HBO's *Rome*, *Spartacus*, and *Band of Brothers*. Men marched, fought, and fell on screen. Empires trembled and collapsed.

The camera cut away from every single one of them eventually, and the story went on. It was a morbid but strangely comforting lesson: no one's suffering, however grand, was the whole story.

None of this counted as triumph. It was maintenance. But it made staying alive feel more possible.

On Christmas Day, 2011, I woke up in the Gerrard Street apartment feeling something I had not felt in a very long time. Rested. Clear. Quiet inside.

The night before, I had been with Walter and Victor's family in Kitchener—my invitation was an olive branch from a family struggling to express love. My mother was there. We acted happy. We discussed nothing meaningful or important. There had been dinner, conversation, the ordinary chaos of Christmas Eve. Now, alone, back in Toronto, I stepped out onto Gerrard Street into a bright, tolerably cold morning. Snow was falling lightly, softening the edges of the city without obscuring anything.

I headed east. Past Yonge, past Church, past Jarvis, toward Parliament. The city felt hushed, emptied of its usual rush. At Parliament, I ducked into Tim Hortons, ordered a coffee, and walked on, cup warming my hand against the cold.

I found myself on the wooded, winding trail behind Riverdale Farm. The Don Valley yawned below, a strip of white and bare trees threading through the city. I crossed a small bridge and stopped in the middle.

For a moment, there was nothing to do. I stood there, breathing in the cold air, feeling the snow land on my face. I tilted my head back and looked up at the bright winter sky, flakes floating down toward me like a slow, silent blessing.

I cannot remember a day, before or since, when I have felt more content or at peace. There was no epiphany, no booming voice. Just a deep, surprising steadiness. An inner stillness I used to imagine was reserved for other people.

By the end of my walk, before turning back toward Gerrard Street, a thought came that did not feel like the old ambition, but like a decision. I would run for President of the Ontario Bar Association. Not for the prestige of the title. I had worn titles and nearly died under their weight. This time, I wanted something different: a platform from which I might be able to help others in some meaningful way.

What that help would look like was a question for another day. On that Christmas morning, it was enough to know that, for the first time in a long time, my ambition was aimed not at escaping myself, but at offering myself, broken history and all, as part of the work.

The snow kept falling. I finished my coffee, turned back toward the city, and walked home. The search for meaning was no longer abstract. I was trying, in my own flawed way, to turn pain into purpose.

One of the places that search led me was north, to Sudbury, to an inquest, and to a pen I'd forgotten I was still carrying.

Chapter 29

The Pen

> *We are what we pretend to be, so we must be careful about what we pretend to be.*
>
> — Kurt Vonnegut, *Mother Night*

SUDBURY IS five hours north of Toronto by car, far enough that the air changes. The highway narrows: the rock cuts rise on either side, and the billboards thin out to the essentials: fuel, food, a reminder about moose crossings. By the time you reach the city, you have driven through enough trees and granite to feel you've left the city orbit and entered a different world.

I was there to represent the Ontario Provincial Police at a coroner's inquest. Inquests sit in a strange corner of the legal world. They are not criminal trials. No one is being sentenced. No one is formally found guilty. The dead have already done the only irreversible thing they can do. The task is narrower and heavier: to stand in a room and ask, in publicly careful language, how the system failed one person, and what might be done so the next person has a better chance.

The man at the center of this inquest was very small. He was barely able to see over the steering wheel of his car. He lived with advanced Chronic Obstructive Pulmonary Disease (COPD) and used supplemental oxygen, a clear plastic line feeding his lungs from a humming tank beside him. He also smoked.

On the day that mattered, he had been in contact with almost everyone who could have saved him. Medical staff had seen him at a hospital and watched him leave against their better judgment. Police officers had stopped him more than once as he wove slightly on the road, concerned enough to pull him over but not enough to pull him off the highway for good. He told them he was going home to a place north of Sudbury, and then on to Toronto to see his son. He never arrived. He died when his car veered off the road.

By the time we were all gathered in the hearing room—coroner, counsel, police witnesses, hospital administrators—the facts were not in dispute. He had died alone on the side of the road, in his car, the tank still humming quietly beside him. The question was not whether the system had failed him, but how many different parts of it had done so, and at what precise points they had each decided to let him carry on.

The hotel conference room, once rearranged, looked like any other hearing room, but its atmosphere was different. We were not arguing over liability or damages or guilt. We were participating in a kind of civic autopsy, opening the body of the system itself to see which organs had failed and why.

I represented the Ontario Provincial Police. Across from me sat counsel for the municipal police service. It was a face I knew well. Murray Segal. Years earlier, he had been my Deputy Attorney General. Before that, he had been the province's lead criminal prosecutor, a central figure in the prosecution of crimes committed in the early nineties. Everyone of a certain age, especially women, remembered the terror of the Scarborough Rapist, later identified as Paul Bernardo. The time was also marked by the disappearance of young teenage girls whom he had raped, murdered, dismembered, and discarded in the Niagara region. He kept videos. Before the video tapes were disclosed to the police, Murray signed off on a plea deal with Bernardo's wife, Karla Homolka, that many criticized. The extent of her knowledge and involvement was not yet clear, and her evidence seemed necessary to convict Bernardo. The plea deal made sense through the lens of a battered-spouse narrative. But long after Murray concluded the deal, Bernardo's lawyer produced video tapes of the crimes. They showed, in graphic, unforgettable horror, the grotesque sadistic harm Bernardo inflicted on his victims. They also revealed Karla Homolka's calculated descent into unspeakable darkness and cruelty.

Murray carried the weight of the decisions, outcomes, and compromises made in the trial of Paul Bernardo and the guilty plea negotiated with Karla Homolka. With hindsight made possible by the video tapes, that plea deal became known as "the deal with the devil." After a long and distinguished career, one that carried on almost twenty years after Bernardo and Homolka were imprisoned, Murray retired on May 31, 2012 in a role that honored his formidable talents, as Deputy Attorney General of Ontario. In time, he returned to private practice, some litigation and some consulting.

Now we sat next to each other at the counsel table, each speaking for a different police service, both trying to help the coroner understand how a very small man with bad lungs and an oxygen tank had been allowed to simply drive himself out of the story.

During a break between witnesses, I reached into my bag for a pen. My fingers closed around the reassuring companion of my courtroom battles, a good luck charm of sorts, and pulled out the black barrel and silver trim of my Montblanc; a pen Adrienne gave me on my thirty-seventh birthday in April 2005. It was also the pen that sat on the Deputy Attorney General's desk during my first nervous briefing with him in January 2006.

For reasons that had been unclear to me until the spring of 2018, during the inquest in Sudbury, at the age of fifty, I carried two identical Montblanc pens.

After my first meeting with Murray back in January 2006, I left his office with my notes, my anxiety, and, unknowingly, his pen. Weeks later, reaching into the pocket of my overcoat on the way into work, I had pulled out not one but two matching pens. They were indistinguishable in my hand. The only difference was three small letters engraved near the cap of one: *MDS*.

I had spent days trying to solve the riddle of MDS. I asked around the office if anyone had lost a good pen. No one came forward. I searched through the Government of Ontario telephone directory, thousands of MSs, but no MDS, middle names or initials were not commonly included. It never occurred to me that the initials belonged to the man at the top of the org chart, who I referred to, not by his name, but respectfully and consistently as "the Deputy." I put both pens in my pocket and kept walking. One had been a birthday gift that stayed in my life longer than the woman who gave it to me. The other had once lived on the desk of the province's top criminal lawyer, future Deputy Attorney General, and now colleague at the counsel table in Sudbury. I treated them interchangeably.

In that Sudbury hotel hearing room, twelve years later, I realized I was still carrying the one with MDS etched into the metal. In the pause between witnesses, I leaned toward Murray David Segal, careful not to tip the stack of binders and a Styrofoam cup of coffee between us.

"I think this belongs to you," I said, suddenly and finally realizing what MDS stood for and placed the pen on the table in front of him.

He looked down, then up at me, and laughed in disbelief.

"Where did you get that?" he asked.

"From your office... about twelve years ago. I guess I'm a slow thief," I said.

"This makes me question your emotional intelligence", he said with a lightness of tone. *Indeed*, I thought.

He tried to wave it off, told me to keep it, and insisted it didn't matter. I insisted harder. It felt wrong to keep carrying someone else's name in my pocket when the owner was sitting beside me. In the end he took it back, still laughing, the way only lawyers can laugh in the middle of something deadly serious: grateful for any excuse to be briefly human.

We laughed about it for days, in the hallway and in the hotel lobby at night, two men whose careers had intersected at different levels of the same institution, passing a joke back and forth like a less dangerous kind of evidence. Returning the pen did not change the outcome of the inquest. It did not resurrect a man, who stood less than five feet tall, or undo the series of decisions that had allowed him to drive when his lungs and judgment were not up to the task. It did not retroactively alter any plea or verdict from the early nineties. It was, on one level, nothing more than a piece of borrowed property finally making its way home.

Still, as I walked back to my side of the room, it was hard not to feel that I had been carrying more than a writing instrument. For years I had been carrying a small, tangible symbol of a kind of authority I had both craved and mistrusted: the authority to sign off on narratives that would be accepted as official truth. The authority to agree to plea bargains, however unpopular in hindsight. The pen I had treated as interchangeable with my own was engraved, quite literally, with someone else's name; the Deputy Chief Law Officer of Ontario.

Handing it back did not absolve me of anything. It did not remove me from the machinery of inquests, or prosecutions, or policies that classified some deaths as preventable and others as unfortunate but acceptable. It simply made it harder to pretend that I was not part of that machinery too.

In Sudbury, in that hearing room, we were trying to reconstruct the last day of a man's life from charts and notes and recollections. Each witness brought a fragment: the doctor who thought he could manage, the hospital nurse who watched him sign himself out; the constable who pulled him over the first time for swerving; the second officer who pulled him over for the same reason but watched him merge into traffic toward a son he would never see again. Each of them had, at that moment, believed they were doing enough.

One of the lessons of inquests is that systems rarely fail all at once. They fail in increments, in small decisions that make sense to the person making them, in the comfortable fiction that someone else further down the road will intervene more decisively, if necessary. Only when those incremental decisions are lined for closer examination, the pattern emerges. It was the same lesson I had been learning, in different forms, my whole life.

No one choice had made my collapse inevitable. It was the accumulated weight of unspoken despair, of stories I had accepted about my worth uttered by people I loved and trusted, of frames I had allowed to define what counted as success and failure by systems evolved to support and protect themselves.

In Sudbury, we called it a system failure. In my own life, I had called it "character." Standing in that room, with the returned pen sitting a few tables away, I felt again the uncomfortable truth that the law, at its best, is an attempt to tell a more honest story about how something happened and who might have done better. At its worst, it is a way of placing a convenient excuse in front of others and calling it enough.

The inquest would end. Recommendations would be made. Policies about discharging patients with oxygen and driving with COPD would be drafted or revised. Somewhere on a highway between Sudbury and Toronto, a small white cross might have appeared at the side of the road. The man's son would live forever with a searing loss—the accumulation of failures from multiple imperfect systems designed to protect his father and those who use our highways.

I would drive back down the same stretch of highway, past the rock and the trees and the last billboards, toward a city full of other hearings and other failures. I would go on representing institutions that tried, in good faith and bad, to do their jobs. And I would do so with slightly less illusion about who held the pen, and how easy it is to mistake carrying it for owning the truth.

That moment in Sudbury reminded me that complicity and clarity often arrive at the same time. It was one thing to survive despair. It was another to be trusted again with the tools of power, but to use them differently. I left Sudbury with a clearer understanding that the systems I once thought were stories told by others, slowly and silently become stories I helped write.

Back in Toronto, the machinery kept churning, and I kept walking toward the center of it.

Chapter 30

The Platform of Meaning

> *You are not obliged to complete the work, but neither are you free to abandon it.*
>
> — Rabbi Tarfon, *Pirkei Avot*

WHILE THE DECISION came on a small bridge behind Riverdale Farm, the work began at my kitchen table, under a nine-page list of names.

Running for President of the Ontario Bar Association did not begin with the word "President." On paper, the role I was seeking in 2012 was Second Vice-President, a modest title that sounded more like a committee assignment than a turning point. But everyone in the room knew what it meant.

Win Second Vice-President in June 2012, and you stepped onto a ladder that moved on its own: Second Vice-President for a year. Then First Vice-President. Then, in August 2014, President of the OBA for a one-year term, ending in August 2015. Three years of forward motion, if you survived the first step.

The OBA was the largest voluntary association of lawyers in Ontario, with over 16,000 members at the time, a provincial branch of the Canadian Bar Association, itself about 37,000 lawyers strong. The electorate for Second Vice-President was the OBA Council: 224 elected representatives from across the province. Those 224 people would decide whether the man who had once resigned as Treasurer in the middle of his term should be given the keys to the presidency.

I knew something about elections. In 2008, I had knocked on thousands of doors in Kitchener–Conestoga, sold ten-dollar memberships, shaken hands at fall fairs and church suppers, and watched my name appear and disappear on television screens. I had learned, the hard way, that there are no shortcuts. People who feel taken for granted do not vote for you. People who feel seen might.

Now, in 2012, the electorate was smaller, but the ask was more personal. I was not just requesting a vote. I was asking for trust in someone whose story contained a large, silent crater in my 2009 resignation.

The official explanation had been health. It was technically true and wholly incomplete. I had kept my depression and anxiety hidden since I was nine years old. I hid it from teachers, friends, colleagues, my own family. Only Jelena and Adrienne had seen enough of the wreckage to put a name to it. Not even my mother seemed to know. When I disappeared into the hospital, the nurses took everything from me—clothes, wallet, keys, phone, anything with weight or an edge—and my life from that point on became a set of careful fictions.

To my family, I said I had been travelling, pretending, as we always did, to keep the peace. To my workplace, I said it was a physical problem. I told no one about the suicide attempt. No one about the ward. No one about the ECT. I was terrified of the stigma.

A lawyer, especially a trial lawyer, is supposed to be strong. People hand you their most important battles, the ones they cannot fight for themselves. How could they trust someone who admitted that, at his lowest, he could not even be trusted with his own life?

I was afraid my friends would step back. Afraid my family would love me less or love me differently. Afraid colleagues would see me not as resilient, but as weak.

I thought about my great-grandfather, dead by suicide in Angola, his true cause of death buried for decades under a different story. I thought about my father's friend in 1979, the man whose funeral I had attended as a boy without being told what had happened. Their deaths had been wrapped in euphemism and silence, as if the worst thing you could do after a suicide was name it. Now I was repeating the pattern: treating my depression as a private shame.

I was campaigning for a leadership role while hiding the central fact of my recent life. But the idea of walking into OBA Council and saying, before 224 members, "I tried to die," felt unimaginable. I could not picture it without also picturing doors closing, eyes averted, chairs pulled back from tables. And I had no intention of changing that—not yet. The fear was too great. The cost felt absolute.

But there was one thing I could do honestly. I could put in the work.

The list of Council members ran nine pages. Names and numbers from every corner of the province: Bay Street towers and Thunder Bay, Windsor and Ottawa, towns I had once passed on school buses and Greyhounds. I printed the list and spread it out on my kitchen table like a map.

I set myself a rule: I would call every Council member and speak, but mostly listen, to anyone willing to pick up.

The first few calls were awkward. "Hi, it's Orlando Da Silva calling. I'm running for Second Vice-President of the OBA..."

The words sounded grander than I felt. Three years earlier, everything I owned had been taken from me at a nurses' station. Now I was asking to be trusted with an entire association. But this was not a confession tour. It was a listening campaign.

"I'm calling to ask for your support," I would say. "More importantly, I'd like to hear what matters to you. What do your members need from the OBA? What do you need?" Then I would shut up.

Some conversations lasted five minutes. Some lasted half an hour. People talked about court delays, legal aid, diversity, burnout, the shrinking middle class of the profession, the loneliness of sole practice. They talked about regions feeling ignored, about young lawyers drowning in debt, about senior lawyers feeling pushed aside.

A few mentioned my resignation in careful, neutral tones. "You stepped down as Treasurer a few years ago," one councilor said. "Are you in a place now where you can take this on?"

"I had a serious health issue and needed to step back," I replied, sticking to the official line. "I took the time I needed. I'm well. If I didn't believe I could serve, I wouldn't be running."

It was the truth, just not the whole truth. The parts that involved kitchen floors and wards stayed where they had always been, inside my head and in a few medical files.

But no one pressed. Some were enthusiastic. Some were cautious. A few were politely noncommittal. Every conversation, even the cool ones, made the election feel less abstract. These were people with different worries and different hopes, trying to decide who they wanted at the front of their organization.

At night, after my voice was hoarse and my ear ached from the phone, I wrote. Not email. Not typed form letters. Handwritten notes. One for each of the 224 Council members. I sat at the table on Gerrard Street with a stack of cards and watched my handwriting loosen as the hours went on, a small smear of ink along the side of my hand as proof.

Dear [Name],

Thank you for taking the time to speak with me...

Each note was specific. I mentioned their town, their practice area, the issue they had raised. I thanked the northern lawyer for explaining how thinly stretched his judicial district was. I thanked the Windsor family lawyer for her candor about burnout. I thanked the skeptical ones for their honesty.

The campaign had all the usual surface elements—posters, buttons, pamphlets, pins. My face reappeared on glossy stock. A designer produced a slogan. Volunteers wore my name on their lapels. It looked like any other OBA election. But for me, the campaign lived in those phone calls and those cards. Every dial, every sentence, was a small act of defiance against the part of me that still believed I had forfeited the right to be trusted.

Past Presidents lent their names. My friend and mentor, Ian Kirby, who had served as OBA President in 2004–2005, offered his endorsement. Others followed. Their support did not erase my resignation, but it reframed it. To them, I was not a punchline or a cautionary tale. I was someone who had gone down, done something about it, and come back.

The speeches and the first round of voting took place on June 12, 2012 at the OBA Conference Centre at 10 Toronto Street, a seven-minute walk east from Scotia Plaza. Council members who attended in person cast their ballots that day. Those who could not attend had thirty days to send in their votes by mail.

I walked to 10 Toronto Street from 720 Bay, files still in my bag. The route was one I had taken countless times for CLE programs and committee meetings. That day, every step felt magnified.

The conference center was filled with the low murmur of lawyers greeting one another. Council members around tables of eight. My face, printed on glossy stock, stared back at them with a friendly and competent countenance. There was the clink of coffee cups, the rustle of agendas, the shuffle of bodies settling in as I took my place at the front near the other candidates.

As the current president called the meeting to order, the familiar physical symptoms arrived: dry mouth, racing heart, a light tremor in my hands. My mind supplied unhelpful comparisons.

In 2008, I stood in a packed hall in Kitchener and watched my federal numbers go up and then stall. This room was smaller, but the stakes did not feel smaller to me. Losing here would not just be a professional setback. It would feel like confirmation that my worst fears about myself were true.

When it was my turn to speak, I walked to the podium. I had written and rewritten my comments for weeks, trying to find the right balance between confidence and humility, direction and listening. In the end, I spoke less from notes than from memory.

I talked about the OBA as a lifeline for isolated lawyers, a defender of the public interest, a voice for those without one. I spoke about my years on Council, my previous time as Treasurer, and the priorities I wanted to pursue, strengthening regional engagement, advocating for better supports for lawyers, deepening the OBA's voice on justice issues that affected real people, not just statutes and systems.

On the question of my resignation, I stayed within the lines I had drawn for myself. "A few years ago, I stepped back from the role of Treasurer for health reasons," I said. "It was the right decision at the time. I took the time I needed. I am grateful to be able to stand here today and ask for your trust again."

I did not say, "depression." I did not say, "suicide attempt." I did not say, "hospital." Even now, with a platform in reach, my fear of those words was stronger than the urge to confess. But lawyers are trained to read between the lines, and I let them.

I finished by telling Council that, whatever they decided, the OBA mattered deeply to me—that it had given me community and purpose when I needed both most—and that I wanted to give that back. Then I thanked them, sat down, and surrendered the rest to the ballot box.

Ballots were distributed to those in the room. Heads bent. Pens marked Xs in small squares. The papers were collected and carried out. For the next thirty days, envelopes would arrive by mail from Council members who hadn't been able to attend in person. Somewhere, my name would be read and tallied against another's.

In 2008, the results had been broadcast on national television. In 2012, there were no cameras, no scrolling graphics. Just a conference room, a stack of ballots, and the space in which my future might tilt one way or another.

While the votes trickled in, another question moved in and refused to leave. If I won, what would I do with it?

There were safe answers. I could attract new members, build on the foundations of past presidents, chair committees, host dinners, visit lawyer associations across the province, and, after a respectable year, hand the association to my successor as tidy as I had received it.

The only thing I could not abide was being a purely custodial president, a careful caretaker who polished the silver, straightened the portraits, and left not a single mark of his own. I did not want the job just to have had it.

The more I turned it over, the more one possibility glared at me from the edge of my vision: using the presidency to talk openly about depression and anxiety in the profession. To break, in public, the code my family and my profession had observed for generations.

Every time that thought surfaced, I shoved it back down. To do that, I would have to tell the truth about Old Carriage Drive. I would have to say the words I had never said, not to my mother, not to my brothers, not to colleagues. I would have to swallow my terror that people would see me as weak, untrustworthy, less worthy of love and confidence.

That decision to confess or not sat like a weight on the table beside my journal, unsolved. I campaigned, spoke, and wrote notes with that unresolved question humming in the background: if I was given a platform, would I dare use it for the one thing that terrified me most?

The ballots were counted. Challenges, if any, were resolved. On July 12, 2012, I was at the Eaton Centre when my phone rang. The number on the display was from the OBA.

"Orlando," said Paul Sweeney, the OBA President, now Justice Sweeney of the Superior Court of Justice. "I'm calling with good news. You've been elected Second Vice-President."

"I don't believe you," I said. The words hung in the air, drowned out by the mall's Muzak and the distant chime of a cash register. There was a brief pause, then a small chuckle.

"What happened to your confidence?" he asked.

I didn't have an answer. Confidence had always been a costume with me, something I put on for other people's benefit. Standing in the middle of a mall, surrounded by stores and strangers and the ordinary noise of commerce, it felt thinner than ever.

We ended the call and I sat down on a bench and stared at my hands as the news began to sink in. I won.

In two years', time, unless something went badly wrong, I would be President of the Ontario Bar Association. The ladder was no longer theoretical. I was standing on its rungs.

The old reflex whispered that they had made a mistake. That if they knew the full story, they would never have put me in this position.

Another voice, quieter but more insistent, answered: They chose you even knowing what they know. The rest is yours to decide.

Sitting there in the Eaton Centre, with shoppers flowing around me and my phone cooling in my hand, the decision I had been circling finally hardened into shape. I would, somehow, use that year to tell the truth about the mind that had almost killed me.

I did not know how I would do it. I did not know how my family would react, or my colleagues, or the Council. I did not know how to square my terror of stigma with the conviction that silence was killing people like me. I only knew that at some point during that term I would have to break the pattern that had buried my great-grandfather and surrounded my father's friend in euphemism. I would have to say aloud what I had only ever written in my journal.

For now, I stood up from the bench, joined the flow of people through the mall, and walked back out into the city. I had failed to die. I had been handed a platform I had never imagined. And somewhere between Gerrard Street West and 10 Toronto Street, between Riverdale Farm and the Eaton Centre, my ambitions had changed.

It was no longer aimed at proving I belonged. It was aimed, however clumsily, at building a room where others like me wouldn't have to disappear.

Chapter 31

The Code Breaker

> *The truth will set you free. But first, it will make you miserable.*
>
> — attributed to James A. Garfield

THE DECISION I made on a bench in the Eaton Centre in June 2012 left me with two years to retreat from it before my term as President began. By the time I became President of the Ontario Bar Association in August 2014, I hadn't budged. I would use the role to tell the truth about the mind that had almost killed me.

At least, in theory. In practice, the old fear never left the room. For those two years as Second and then First Vice-President, that unresolved decision travelled with me from council meetings to bar dinners. I had drafted a one-page list of safe, anodyne priorities for my term. Mental health wasn't on it. Keeping my secret was Priority Zero.

I had grown up in a family where suicide was something that happened offstage and was never named, at least until after I had disclosed my own attempt. Now I was President of an association in a profession that prided itself on clarity and precision, and I was still living by the same vague code. I knew I wanted to break it. I just didn't know how. That opening came, almost by accident, in a boardroom.

Not long after my term began, the OBA's Director of Communications, Greg Cone, arranged an interview with a reporter from *Law Times*. She and I met in a boardroom at the OBA Conference Centre. A rectangular table, a jug of water, a notepad, a small digital recorder with a blinking red light.

We started with the usual questions.

What did I hope to accomplish as president? What were my priorities? What did I see as the biggest issues facing the profession? I talked about the things every OBA President talks about, like access to justice, diversity, regional engagement, and the pressures on young lawyers and on legal aid.

Then she asked, almost casually, "Is there anything in your own story that informs the way you see this role?"

There was a safe answer. I could have talked about being the child of immigrants, about Weber Street, about being the first in my family to go to university. I could have repeated the well-sanded anecdotes of resilience that draw applause, but not much else.

Instead, I heard myself say, "Yes. I live with major depression." The room did not change. The bottled water and coffee stayed where it was. Her pen kept moving across the notepad. The recorder's tiny red light kept blinking. I went on.

I told her that no one at work had known, that no one in my family knew, that I had been off the edge of the map and pulled back. I did not give every detail, but I gave enough: a suicide attempt, hospitalization, treatment, a return. My hands were steady on the table. My voice was calm. Inside, every instinct screamed that I was detonating my career in a trade publication.

A short time later, *Law Times* ran the story. It was not front-page news. It did not trend. But it landed exactly where it needed to: on the desks and screens of lawyers across Ontario, and in the hands of a reporter at the *Toronto Star* named Jim Coyle.

The Star called. Jim wanted to write about the President of the Ontario Bar Association who was prepared to talk openly about his depression and suicide attempt. We spoke at length, and he asked the questions I had spent my life avoiding: When did it start? How bad did it get? What stopped you? Why tell this story now?

I told him about the kitchen floor at Old Carriage Drive. I told him about the ward, the ECT, the journal, the ten-point scale I used to track my mood. I told him about thinking of my death as an act of love, a way to relieve my family of the burden of me. We talked about law, too, about a profession that valorizes invulnerability and stoicism, one that still whispers "weakness" behind the backs of those who break down.

On September 2, 2014, his article appeared. I read it once online, heart pounding, then again in print, as if seeing it on paper might make it less real. My story, my family's story, was now a public artifact, folded into coffee shops and left on subway seats.

My phone lit up. Text messages from colleagues. Emails from judges. Notes from old friends. Some were a single line, "Me too," from people I had never suspected were carrying their own versions of my story. Others were long paragraphs of gratitude, relief, and anger at a system that had made them feel alone.

Then my daughter called. Candace was sixteen. Her voice came down the line sharp and hurt. "You've ruined my life," she said. "You've ruined my career." I sat with the phone in my hand after she hung up, not moving. I had spent years calculating the cost of silence, what it did to people who hid their illness, what it had done to me. I had not fully calculated the cost of speaking. In her world, grade eleven and twelve, reputations were fragile and merciless. Her father's suicide attempt, laid out in the province's largest newspaper, felt like a stain that would spread onto her. I had spent years hiding my illness to protect the people I loved. Now, in telling the truth, I had wounded the most important one among them. I had imagined stigma coming from the profession and the public. I hadn't prepared to deliver that stigma like a thunderclap to my child. In the midnight hours above the lake, I had promised her that I would never hurt her the way I had been hurt. The promise was sincere. It was also not enough.

At home, my mother read the article. For the first time, seemingly, she learned that her son had tried to die. The conversations that followed are their own chapters. They started a pattern that demanded my immediate attention. Calls or texts had to be returned without hesitation, because, as far as my mother was concerned, silence was evidence of suicidality. Although more than six years had passed since my suicide attempt, I had to reassure her almost daily that I was not about to take my life; I was merely engulfed in the busy demands of work and parenting. Something about her insistent demands for reassurance and comfort irked me, but I couldn't name why. For now, what mattered was this: I had said the thing aloud in a way that could not be taken back. The secret that had shaped my life since childhood was no longer mine alone to carry. Silence had been our family's strategy for survival. Now, whether we liked it or not, the silence was broken.

The article did something else I hadn't anticipated. It turned me into a person organizations wanted on a stage. Not long after the *Toronto Star* piece ran, the Association of Law Officers of the Crown —ALOC, which represents Ontario's civil Crown lawyers—invited me to speak at their annual retreat at the White Oaks Resort and Spa near Niagara-on-the-Lake. I was a member of ALOC myself. I knew the crowd: smart, driven, often exhausted lawyers who spent their days defending the Crown in court and advising the government in boardrooms. The topic they gave me was "Depression in the Workplace."

On the day of the retreat, I arrived at White Oaks and was shown to an anteroom beside the largest conference space. About 800 government lawyers sat at round tables in the main hall, their backs to me, their attention fixed on the stage. On it, Chantal Hébert, a journalist and frequent political commentator on CBC, was speaking about accountability in the public sector. I stood in the wings and listened. Her words were sharp, precise, unsparing. The crowd was rapt. When she finished, the room erupted in applause.

As she stepped down, people began to stand and stretch. On the edge of the stage, ALOC President Sean Hanley turned to me with a smile that tried to be reassuring and said, "You're up." My knees, for a moment, considered other options.

Eight hundred of my colleagues sat on the other side of the curtain. Some knew me as a litigator, some as a bureaucrat, some now as the OBA President from the *Star* article. Many didn't know me at all. All of them, I knew, had been trained in the same culture of competence and control.

Sean walked up to the podium, thanked Chantal, and introduced me. I watched her pack her notes into her bag as my name echoed through the sound system.

I stepped onto the stage and crossed what felt like an impossible distance to the lectern. The room was vast: rows of round tables disappearing into the back, the hum of side conversations dying down. The lights were bright enough that I could see only the first few rings of faces clearly.

I gripped the sides of the lectern, willed my legs to hold, and thanked them for inviting me to speak "after Chantal Hébert." It was meant as a joke. Thankfully, they took it as one. The room laughed. I went on.

"Given the topic," I said, "it's only natural that 'Depression in the Workplace' would follow 'Accountability in the Public Sector'."

This time they roared.

The laughter broke something open, for them and for me. It bought me a few seconds to breathe, to remember why I was there.

Then I told them the biggest secret of my life. I told them about the ten-point scale. Seven is functional. Four is dangerous. About the journal where depression claimed to be permanent and the blank spaces called it a liar. About isolation being gasoline on the fire.

"It can convince you," I said, my voice finding a groove in the acoustics of that room, "that your death would be the greatest act of love you could offer." I saw heads nodding at some of the tables. Others were very still.

I didn't turn the talk into a medical lecture. I talked about what I did, practically, to resist the spiral: forcing myself to exercise when I didn't want to; to walk outside when the apartment felt like a coffin; to have coffee or lunch with a friend when every instinct told me to cancel. Each small act was a handhold on the way down.

"I am not here to tell you to stand on a stage in front of hundreds of people and talk about your darkest moments," I said. "Believe me, I would not recommend this as a first step."

The room laughed again, softer this time.

"What I am hoping," I continued, "is that by telling you my story, it might make it easier for you to tell yours, to a friend, a relative, a counselor, a doctor, anyone. Because here is the good news: for those who have depression and seek help, as many as eighty percent get better. Not overnight. Not perfectly. But better."

I let the number hang in the air. Eighty percent. In a profession that worships winning percentages, it was a statistic that sounded, to me, like hope.

When I finished, there was a brief, heavy silence. Then hundreds of government lawyers, people who had been trained to keep a straight face under cross-examination, to fold their feelings into footnotes, rose to their feet and applauded.

From the stage, the sound washed over me in a way I had not expected. It did not feel like approval of a performance. It felt like recognition. Like the noise a room makes when a secret they have all been keeping, in different forms, is finally named.

Lunch was next on the agenda. It didn't start on time. A line formed at the front of the room and along the side aisles, people waiting to speak, or to shake my hand, or just to stand close enough to say, "Thank you" and then retreat before their voices broke.

I stayed for forty-five minutes and spoke with everyone who wanted or needed to talk. Some said a few words and moved on. Some whispered "me too" and stopped. Others told me pieces of their own stories: panic attacks hidden in washrooms between hearings, medication bottles tucked in desk drawers, nights spent on couches staring at ceilings, spouses who didn't know, bosses who wouldn't understand.

Eventually, the line thinned. Plates clattered in the distance. The smell of lunch drifted in from another room. I slipped away, grabbed my coat from the rack, and almost ran for the parking lot, stopped again and again by people who had heard me speak and wanted one more sentence, one more piece of the story, one more assurance that they were not alone.

I drove home eastbound on the QEW in a daze, replaying every moment of the speech, every intake of breath, every face in the first few rows. When I reached home and took my coat off, I realized, slowly, with a flush of embarrassment, that it wasn't mine. It fit well enough, but it was the wrong color and a significant upgrade. Instead of my dull gray trench coat, I was wearing a deep olive London Fog. I had left carrying a stranger's better coat.

I checked the pockets, found no identification, and hung it up in my hallway, a visual joke at my own expense. I had stolen, unwittingly, the outer shell of a more put-together man.

Then I checked my email. I received hundreds of messages. More on social media. Reactions to the *Star* article and to the ALOC speech, arriving in the same digital rush: Crown counsel, private practitioners, articling students, senior partners, law students, judges, people I had never met and would never meet.

Some wrote at length. Some wrote one line. Many said some version of: "I thought I was the only one," or "Because of what you said today, I am going to talk to someone," or simply, "Thank you. I am still here."

The cost of breaking the code was real. It was evident in my daughter's anger, my family's shock, and the permanent vulnerability of walking into every new room knowing people knew the worst day of my life before they knew anything else about me.

But the cost of keeping it was a life lived in a lie. The illness that had disqualified me in my own mind had become, impossibly, the qualification.

I was no longer a president with a secret. I was a witness with a platform.

Chapter 32

"Please, Mom. Don't Tell Anyone"

> *In the end, we will remember not the words of our enemies, but the silence of our friends.*
>
> — Martin Luther King, Jr.

KOERNER HALL WAS BUILT for celebration. The world-renowned, 1,135-seat performance venue—warm wood curves, exceptional acoustics, intimate sightlines—had hosted some of the finest musicians in the world. On a night in April 2016, it was packed to honor Paul Beeston, the former President of the Toronto Blue Jays during their back-to-back World Series wins in 1992 and 1993, and later President of Major League Baseball. The stage was set for triumph with a hall tuned for applause, an audience of executives, lawyers, physicians, athletes, and guests dressed for a night out.

Koerner Hall smelled of polished wood and ambition. They'd paid for a high-end celebration. I was there to talk about the mind's mutiny. They asked me to come and talk about losing, about depression and suicide.

By then, I'd been telling my story in rooms far less glamorous for two years. Each time, I walked to the microphone with the same two voices in my head: the old one, asking who I thought I was to speak at all, and the newer one, saying, this is why you're here.

Koerner Hall added a third: Don't ruin the night.

But I spoke anyway.

I talked about the mind that can't stop rehearsing ways to die. About the ten-point scale and the journal. About isolation as gasoline. About lawyers who looked fine in daylight and disintegrated alone. I did what I had done in so many other rooms: took the worst day of my life and held it up under good lighting, hoping it might do someone else some good. The acoustics were as advertised. You could hear every breath.

Afterwards, in the lobby, people lined up in that familiar way: polite, practiced, a post-speech receiving line. They shook my hand, made quick eye contact, said, "Thank you," or "That was brave," or, "I had no idea," and drifted back into clusters around the bar.

One woman in her forties stepped a little out of the line looking tentative. We made eye contact. I nodded. She waited until there was no one directly behind us.

"My daughter died by suicide shortly before Christmas," she said. "She was fourteen." Her voice sounded both practiced and about to break.

The air between us shifted. The hall noise receded to a muffled wash.

"She left a note," the mother said. She didn't cry. She stated it. A fact. "Please Mom, don't tell anyone."

Around us, the lobby hummed with the low, satisfied frequency of a successful night. That sentence, in that hall, was a sound from a different universe.

I had heard versions of my own story in dozens of voices by that point. Panic in washrooms. Pills in desk drawers. Sleepless nights. Spouses kept in the dark. Parents who still didn't know. But this was different.

Fourteen years old. Just before Christmas. "Please Mom, don't tell anyone." The words landed like an echo from another age.

My great-grandfather, who died in Angola, and was buried in a proper Catholic Cemetery. He had had his cause of death white-washed, rewritten, and retold. In 1979, my father's best childhood friend was buried without a Mass, a prayer, or a word in an unmarked communal grave, because he rejected God's greatest gift, his life, and died by suicide. My own attempt on that kitchen floor had been recast as "health reasons" and "time away."

Here it was again, distilled to a single plea, written by a young girl, expressing her dying wish: "Please Mom, don't tell anyone."

The request was, in its own way, an act of love. She wanted to spare her mother embarrassment, pity, the scrutiny of neighbours, the gossip of classmates' parents. She had absorbed, at fourteen, the lesson it had taken me decades to unlearn: that the worst thing you could do with pain is let other people see it.

Standing there in Koerner Hall, in a suit on a good night, I realized that everything I'd been doing since that first *Law Times* interview was, fundamentally, a refusal to honor that command. In that moment, my advocacy inverted. It was no longer about my right to speak. It was about our duty to listen, and to disobey. To hear "don't tell" and understand it as a symptom of the very sickness we were sworn to treat.

We have created a world where secrecy is a reasonable request. We teach it without meaning to. Don't talk about that. Don't upset your mother. Don't shame the family. Don't jeopardize your career or ruin mine. Don't let clients lose their confidence in your advocacy. Don't give employers a reason to think you're unstable. Don't make anyone uncomfortable. Don't show weakness. Don't tell anyone anything. *Ever.*

We then act surprised when people in deep distress choose silence over help.

That fourteen-year-old girl's note rebooted my understanding of the work. The right I was fighting for was not just my right to speak.

It was the right, and sometimes the obligation, of people who loved someone in trouble to speak, too. To break the secrecy that was killing them. To say, it's not a betrayal if I tell the truth about what you're going through. It's an act of care.

That night, the thought I had been carrying in my head for this part of my life shifted into focus. We must *not* remain silent. I developed my voice, and overcame my fear of using it, for this moment.

Out of those conversations came something small on its face and larger in its implications: an initiative created by the Ontario Bar Association, for the benefit of professionals suffering in silence. We called it "Opening Remarks" to signal the beginning of the discussion about mental health in the legal profession. We created a vault of interviews with prominent lawyers and doctors; daily "Wellness Tips," supplied by the Ontario Psychology Association; a "Mindful Lawyer Series" of courses on mental wellness in the profession. All these tools were accessible free of charge and have been watched by tens of thousands of lawyers in Ontario, across Canada, and around the world. Given its reach, quality, and importance, OBA's Opening Remarks was recognized with national and international awards. It became our standard bearer for the message that we would stop treating mental illness as a private defect and start treating it as part of our shared professional reality and mutual obligation.

At OBA events, instead of shunting mental health to a side panel, an optional "wellness break," or a rarely visited conference booth, someone in authority would acknowledge, in their own words, that mental health challenges are common in our profession. That help is available. That talking about these issues is welcome. That if you are struggling, you are not alone and you are not a liability.

We were aiming for a steady, repeated signal amplifying a new reality— the subject was no longer taboo and that the pretense that depression wasn't already present in the room, indeed, in every room, had to stop.

The awkwardness of this endeavor was palpable. I still cringe thinking about moments standing before my own mic. Some people shifted in their seats. Others looked down at their programs. But after a few events, lawyers began coming up afterward not to talk about the technical content but to say, "Thank you for mentioning that at the start. It made it feel normal." Their relief was disproportionate to the number of words. That was the whole point.

Years later, the OBA would create the *Orlando Da Silva Award for Improvement of Mental Wellbeing in the Justice Sector*, recognizing sustained efforts to address mental health in our world. The name on the award matters less to me than what it represents: that "Opening Remarks" stopped being just my project and became part of how the profession understands its duty of care to its own.

At the Ministry of the Attorney General, Beth Beattie and I shared a stage at an event organized by a group we co-founded called "Voices of Mental Health." Two senior lawyers, both with serious illnesses of the mind, speaking plainly in a place where illness was usually treated as private weakness or an HR problem. We talked about diagnosis and medication, but also about performance reviews, courtroom appearances, and the practical fear that if anyone found out, our careers would evaporate. We said, out loud, the quiet calculations we knew dozens of people in that room were making every day.

On Bay Street, the firms that had shown me the door in 1991 began inviting me back. This time, it wasn't to be judged for hire back potential. It was to speak to their partners and associates about the thing they had always suspected was there and never quite knew how to name. I stood at lecterns in boardrooms with skyline views and breathtaking lake views and talked about kitchen floors and hospital gowns.

Some private-sector businesses offered between five thousand and twenty-five thousand dollars for a forty-five-minute talk. Every cheque went to Youth Mental Health Canada, founded by my friend Sheryl Boswell.

The invitations spread beyond law, too. I spoke across Canada twice, into the United States, even to audiences in Africa. Rooms of thirty, virtual rooms of seven thousand. Union conferences. Insurance gatherings. Professional associations that had nothing to do with law except that their members were also human.

The stories I heard in those rooms were depressingly similar and strangely hopeful: different professions, same silence; different countries, same shame; different languages, same relief when someone said, "Me too."

My depression never left. It still hasn't. The ten-point scale remains at the ready. The journal, with its clusters of dark ink and long blank stretches, still sits on a shelf. I still have days when the numbers slide, when the thought returns that the kindest thing I could do for the people I love is to vanish.

The difference is that those thoughts no longer feel like private, shameful truths. They feel like symptoms I can name in public without exploding my life.

I didn't wait until I was "cured" to start speaking. I spoke as someone who remained, stubbornly, sick and alive.

The note from that fourteen-year-old girl has never left me. I couldn't save her. None of my speeches could reach backwards in time. Her request to her mother, "Please don't tell anyone"—written in ink I can't erase, sealing an act I can't undo. But, for the next child, for every child, I could and would refuse to contribute to a world that demanded secrecy when compassion was required. Simply put, I speak because she asked for silence. In my small corner of the world, the least I could do was to help create a safe port in the storm, where the loving response to silence founded by shame would be met with a gentle but firm, "No, we must tell someone. You deserve help. You deserve compassion. You deserve love. You deserve to live."

Chapter 33

High-Functioning

> *Ever tried. Ever failed. No matter. Try again. Fail again. Fail better.*
>
> — Samuel Beckett, *Worstward Ho*

On December 18, 2008, I tried to die. Six years later, I became President of the Ontario Bar Association.

During both these events, and for more than ten years after first revealing my affliction, and even until this very moment in fact, I know that my depressive cyclicals continue, returning every few years in episodes lasting six to eighteen months. I never know what triggers them or what relieves them.

During these depressive stretches, my days split in two. There is the part the world sees: the meetings chaired, the memos written, the hearings attended, the speeches delivered with steady voice and eye contact. Then there are the hours after the workday ends, when all meaningful distractions fade and I retreat to a darkened room and think of nothing but when and how to die until exhaustion finally lets me sleep.

The next morning, the alarm goes off. I shower, dress, knot a tie, and step back into the outside half of my life.

Long after my suicide attempt, my recovery from bankruptcy, my return to work as a full-time trial lawyer with the Ministry of the Attorney General, and three months after becoming President of the Ontario Bar Association, I married my wife, Gianna, in December 2014, and became the stepfather of her two young daughters. My eldest daughter, Candace, forgave me for the *Toronto Star* article and together, Gianna and my girls, loved me, not for what I could do, but for who I was. They brought me their happiness and laughter. They shared their fears and hopes. Their love felt undeserved but kept me safe. They learned the shorthand of my ten-point scale. "Where are you today?" they would ask.

Anything above a six meant I was functioning and, in my own strange way, hopeful. A five meant they watched me more closely. Three and below was danger. At three, I could not help myself. I needed them to drag me out to a mall, a Starbucks, a Chapters, anywhere that might interrupt the downward spiral for an hour.

Nothing could replace their love as a means of keeping me alive. They reminded me, repeatedly, that the storm was temporary, despite how permanent it felt. They had watched me emerge before. They believed I would again, even when I couldn't remember ever feeling well.

"A depressed mind lies to you," Gianna would say, sometimes bluntly, sometimes with a joke. "We have the receipts."

I still had my journal. Those same blank stretches that had saved me on Gerrard Street continued to testify against the illusion of permanence. I would read an entry from years earlier—dark, absolute, certain that I would never feel better—and then look at the date and think of all that had happened since. The mind that had written it had been wrong. The illness was persistent, brutal, but not static.

So I would hold on until the storm passed. Sometimes the shift came in small increments; other times I woke up one morning and noticed that the light in the room felt different, as if someone had quietly opened a curtain in the night.

I never knew when a depressive episode would arrive, how long it would last, or what, exactly, would loosen its grip. What I did know was that I had to keep moving anyway.

I had always been high functioning, even at my worst. As an Assistant Crown Attorney in Newmarket, I completed thirty-six trials during a major depressive episode. I won thirty-two of them. I stood up, addressed courts, cross-examined witnesses, closed arguments. In the evenings, I drove home, sat in the dark, and planned my own death. No one in the courthouse could tell.

Helping others with depression, and those who care for them, crystalized a thought that formed when I was released from the psychiatric ward in May 2009: *maybe my mind had always been lying to me about my self-worth.* Maybe I could still give my life purpose, even if happiness remained forever out of reach. Maybe that purpose, or meaning, could give me hope, and maybe that hope could save myself from myself.

Through that lens, returning my day job as a civil litigator at the Ministry of the Attorney General felt like going back to chopping wood—useful but not nourishing. I looked for roles that offered more than a paycheck; jobs that intersected with justice and human beings in ways that felt less abstract. Criminal prosecution helped for a while. Standing in court on behalf of the Crown, I could feel the weight of my work in a way I hadn't in memos and policy drafts. But even that, eventually, began to feel like only part of the answer.

In late 2017, I applied to become a judge of the Superior Court of Justice of Ontario, a longstanding dream. The Toronto selection committee declined to recommend me. I tried to learn why. There are always multiple factors, some of them unknowable, but word filtered back that, considering the stress of the role, the committee "would not be doing me any favors" by recommending me.

The boy forged on Weber Street, the man who had cross-examined organized crime figures and a serial killer in packed courtrooms, who had stood on stages across the country talking about his greatest weakness, was apparently too fragile to sit behind a bench. I was furious. Not because I felt entitled to the robe, but because the very advocacy that had helped others seemed to have been counted against me. The stigma I was trying to dismantle had walked into the room undercover, wearing the language of "concern."

If the door to that life was closed, I needed another one. When the opportunity came to leave the courtroom and lead an organization, I jumped. On the recommendation of Minister of Justice David Lametti, I was appointed Chief Administrator of the Administrative Tribunals Support Service of Canada (ATSSC) by the federal Cabinet. I was responsible for a six-hundred-plus-person organization with a budget in the hundred-million-dollar range, supporting many of Canada's administrative tribunals: court-like bodies that decide disputes touching nearly every realm of human endeavor in this country.

I brought my depression with me. I also brought what it had taught me.

I led with empathy, authenticity, and a deliberate vulnerability, trying to create a psychologically safe and genuinely stigma-free workplace. I had no interest in recreating the toxicity I had inherited. I knew what it felt like to dread going to work and to hide the worst parts of yourself from the people you spent your days with.

With the help of my executive team and some of my fiercest supporters, we pulled the ATSSC out of the ditch. Employee surveys that had once put us near the bottom of the National Capital Region began to climb. Eventually, we were ranked among the top employers in Ottawa, outscoring the public-sector average on every one of the metrics tracked. We saved taxpayers millions per year while still earning a ninety-plus percent satisfaction rating from the tribunals we served. I was reappointed for a second five-year term, this time on the recommendation of Minister of Justice Arif Virani.

These are not the markers of a fairy-tale ending. They are one version of what high-functioning depression can look like when you endure its episodic pain, accept that you may never be "finished" with it, and surround yourself with people who refuse to let it have the last word.

My wife, Gianna, our two daughters, Lizzie and Emily, and my oldest daughter, Candace, are central to that refusal.

A year before I met Gianna, in 2011, I needed emergency surgery to remove my gallbladder. I went first to the emergency department at Toronto General Hospital. After many hours, I was sent back to 40 Gerrard with advice but no treatment. Eight hours later, still in pain, I walked to St. Michael's Hospital. They admitted me, hooked me up to a dextrose-saline IV, and moved me to a corner of the emergency department, far from the nurses' station.

There were several of us waiting there, each absorbed in our own discomfort. An elderly man beside me muttered hoarsely and incoherently as he voided his bowels, nonstop.

The smell was overwhelming. Part of me was amazed it didn't trigger a code blue for the olfactory system alone, let alone attract the care he so clearly needed. By proximity, I shared both his humiliation and his invisibility.

Two full shifts turned before a nurse noticed that my IV bag had run dry long ago. She apologized with real anger at the system that had left us, however unintentionally, to endure in a forgotten corner.

Five days after laparoscopic surgery—an unusually long stay, in part because I had no one at home to care for me—I was discharged back to 40 Gerrard.

Years later, in 2017, I needed surgery again, this time in Guelph. By then, I was married to Gianna.

She, in her loving way, insisted on staying with me. For three days, she slept in the visitors' chair beside my bed, advocating for every medication, every adjustment, every small comfort. Our daughters joined in, a team of love hovering over one patient, their care a constant, loving pressure no overburdened system could ignore.

The contrast between those two recoveries was stark. In 2011, the hospital did its best with limited resources, and I went home to an apartment watched over by no one. In 2017, the hospital still had limits, but I was never invisible. Every nurse and doctor knew there was an Italian wife in the room who intended to see me safely through.

When I think about who is most at risk in any system, including one that offers Medical Assistance in Dying (MAiD) for mental illness, it is not people like me, surrounded now by loving, insistent faces. It is the version of me who lived at Old Carriage Drive and 40 Gerrard Street West. The one recovering alone in an apartment or waiting on a forgotten gurney in a corner of the emergency department. The ones whose absence might look, to an overburdened system, like a small mercy.

The honors I've received, the roles I've held, the measurable improvements at ATSSC, none of these are proof that I've "won." They are proof that a life can be rich, difficult, and meaningful at the same time. A person can be trusted with other people's livelihood and justice even while tracking his own mood on a ten-point scale and occasionally sinking into a three.

If happiness ever arrives as a permanent guest, I will welcome it with gratitude. Until then, I have learned to accept a life that prioritizes meaning and service over mood. Without that, the pain I have suffered, and will continue to suffer, would have no purpose.

The fact that I failed to die in 2008 did not grant me a happily ever after. It gave me something more complicated, and in its own way, more valuable: the chance to live a flawed, unfinished life that still manages to be useful.

That chance is the reason I cannot abide a system that would have offered the 2008 version of me medical assistance in dying when, despite my persuasive protestations, what I really needed, and thankfully received, was medical assistance in *living*.

Epilogue

The Case Against MAiD Where Mental Illness Is the Sole Underlying Medical Condition (SUMC)

> *Have a heart that never hardens, and a temper that never tires, and a touch that never hurts.*
>
> — Charles Dickens, *Our Mutual Friend*

When I hear arguments in favor of Canada's euthanasia and assisted suicide regime expanding to include people whose only underlying condition is mental illness, I think of hallways.

I think of the corridor outside the ECT suite, where beds line up and patients in gowns wait for shocks that might, or might not, loosen the grip of depression on their own minds.

Or the fluorescent hallway of the first ward, crowded with people who want to be admitted because the streets are too cold to survive.

And the narrow hallway at Old Carriage Drive, where my campaign signs leaned against the wall and my body lay on the kitchen floor.

In each of those places, if you had asked me whether I wanted to live, I would have given you a clear, articulate answer. *No.*

I met every proposed criterion for MAiD where mental illness is the sole underlying condition. My illness was longstanding. My suffering was severe. I had tried multiple treatments: antidepressants, sleeping pills, anti-anxiety medications, psychotherapy, later, ECT. I believed—calmly, rationally, convincingly—that I was a burden, that I would never get better, that the kindest thing I could do for the people I loved was to die.

If MAiD had been available then as a "treatment option," delivered by a kind, soft-spoken psychiatrist in a white coat, clipboard in hand, I have little doubt how the conversation might have gone.

"You've been sick for a long time. You've tried many treatments. Your suffering is grievous and, in our view, irremediable. We can offer you one more form of relief."

I would have signed.

Six months later, the facts of my history would have been the same. The childhood. The balcony. Weber Street. The kitchen floor. The ward. The journal. The ten-point scale. The only difference would have been time, safety, and the stubborn refusal of a few professionals, and a few strangers, to accept my certainty as the last word. The depressive episode that had seemed permanent turned out, once again, to be cyclical.

That is the first problem with MAiD where mental illness is the sole underlying condition. The illness itself interferes with the very capacities the law is supposed to protect—judgment, memory, hope.

When I am depressed, I cannot remember *not* being depressed. I cannot imagine a future in which I am not depressed, because the present feels like a verdict, not a phase.

A clinician who met me only in those states would encounter a convincing, intelligent adult, able to explain his reasoning and articulate his values. They would not see the long blank stretches in my journal testifying that the same brain, given enough time and care, had repeatedly proven itself wrong.

A second problem is love. We like to imagine suicide as an act of selfish escape. Often, it is the opposite. In the irrational logic of a depressed mind, it can feel like the ultimate sacrifice.

If I leave, my family will be spared.

If I leave, my colleagues won't have to carry me.

If I leave, the system will have more resources for people who matter.

I have thought all those things.

Layer MAiD onto an underfunded, overwhelmed mental-health system, and that self-sacrifice can start to look disturbingly rational. The person who already believes they are a burden may come to see their death as a gift: fewer appointments, fewer costs, one less file in the queue. They become, in their own minds, a kind of modern version of Dickens' Sydney Carton, stepping forward with a twisted sense of nobility: "It is a far, far better thing that I do, than I have ever done. It is a far, far greater rest that I go to, than I have ever known."

We tell ourselves that capacity assessments and safeguards will sort this out. That clinicians will be able to distinguish between a considered, enduring wish to die and a temporary distortion of illness.

Sometimes they will. Many times, they won't.

Depression is not a tumor you can measure, or a failing organ you can scan. It is a story the brain tells itself—about value, about burden, about future—and insists is fact. The more articulate the patient, the more persuasive the story.

The law requires that a person's condition be "irremediable." In the world of mental illness, that word is less a diagnosis than a bet. We cannot, with any confidence, say who among the living will never improve. We can say, with considerable certainty, that a dead person will never surprise us.

Third, there is the question of support. When I lay on the kitchen floor at Old Carriage Drive, I lived alone. When I staggered through my gallbladder crisis in 2011, I recovered alone. In both cases, my survival depended on strangers doing their jobs, not on any protective net of family.

Years later, in Guelph, I went under the knife again, but this time with an Italian wife sleeping in a hospital chair and three daughters within a text's reach. The hospital still had limits, but I was never invisible. Every doctor and nurse who entered that room knew there were people there who loved me enough to be loudly inconvenient.

If MAiD had been available at Old Carriage Drive, I would have been an ideal candidate: solitary, convinced of my own expendability, eager to relieve the people I loved of the burden I had become. If MAiD had been offered in Guelph, I would have had a room full of witnesses making it clear, if anyone would listen, that removing me would not be an act of mercy.

Which version of me should the law be calibrated for?

Laws like this cannot be built around the luckiest cases: the moments when someone like me is surrounded by love and good care. They must be built for the most vulnerable version of me, the one on the kitchen floor who could explain, calmly and convincingly, he should die. We do not build public policy around the luckiest cases. We build it around the most vulnerable.

The people most at risk under a MAiD regime for mental illness are not the well-resourced, well-connected, well-loved patients with access to therapy, community, and advocacy. They are the ones in forgotten corners of emergency departments, in rented rooms, in student towers that smell of instant noodles and stale beer. The deaths of the most vulnerable amongst us, to a system already buckling under demand, may begin to look more like efficiency and less like medical assistance.

Finally, there is the note from Koerner Hall: "Please Mom, don't tell anyone." A fourteen-year-old girl absorbed, before she was old enough to drive, the belief that the worst thing her mother could do with her pain was speak it aloud. She carried that belief to the grave.

MAiD for mental illness, introduced into a culture that still mistakes silence for strength, will not land on a blank slate. It will land on families who have been taught for generations not to talk. On professions that still treat breakdown as failure. On communities where "getting help" is whispered, if it is mentioned at all.

We may think we are offering autonomy. To many, it will feel like a verdict: You are right. You are a burden. You are beyond help. Here is a clean, clinical way to take yourself out of the equation and free us to care for those who deserve it.

That is exactly how I would see it. When deep in the throes of a depressive episode, I still don't believe I deserve help, let alone love, or even a marked grave.

I am not arguing that there is no such thing as unbearable psychiatric suffering. I have lived close enough to it to know better. I am not suggesting that every story ends like mine. Some people suffer for decades with little relief. Some will die by suicide regardless of what the law says.

What I am arguing is that a society that has not yet done the hard work of providing real, sustained, accessible mental health care has no moral right to offer death as a medical service to the people it failed.

We do not need medical assistance in dying for people like me. We need medical assistance in *living*.

Assistance that looks like:

- Enough inpatient beds that someone in crisis is not warehoused in an emergency hallway for days.
- Adequately funded therapy and community support, so treatment is not limited to pills and waiting lists.
- Housing and income support that make it possible to survive between episodes without falling through every crack.
- Workplaces where programs like "Opening Remarks" are not novelties but norms, and where leaders who admit to struggling are not quietly sidelined.
- Families and communities that understand that saying, "I'm not okay," is not an embarrassment, but an invitation.

Thank God I failed.

If my suicide attempt in 2008 had succeeded, none of the life that followed would exist: not the love of Gianna, not the three daughters I love more than life itself, not the OBA presidency or the tribunal work, not the speeches that led other people to seek help, not the thousands of quiet "me too"s whispered after events.

It would be tempting to tidy this into a redemption story: I suffered, I survived, I spoke, and everything worked out. But that is not my reality.

My depression is still here. It still lies to me. There are still nights when the old thoughts circle back, persuasive as ever. The difference is that I now have evidence, in the form of blank pages and living faces, that those thoughts are not the truth.

The title of this book is no slogan. It is a diagnosis of a system that is about to forget what failure can save.

I failed to die. Because I failed, I was forced into treatment I did not want, surrounded by people I did not ask for, and offered time I did not believe would help. That time turned out to be the difference between a permanent decision and a survivable episode. If we normalize MAiD where mental illness is the sole underlying condition, we will be taking that time away from people whose minds are tormenting them with the same false certainties that once tormented me.

I am not at peace because my illness vanished. I am at peace because, despite it, my life has meaning, and because other people refused to let my worst moments define my future. For those reasons, and for the fourteen-year-old whose last request was a plea for secrecy, I cannot remain silent.

The right I am claiming for myself, and for others like me, is not the right to die when we are sick. It is the right *not* to be offered death as a substitute for the care, love, and patience that keep revealing our minds to be unreliable narrators of our own worth.

Coda: How I Live with Depression

(This is not medical advice. Or legal advice, for that matter.)

On the night of March 6, 2026, at Gianna's suggestion, I went to bed early in the hope that sleep might quiet the depressive thoughts that had been reducing me to rubble. Gianna was still up organizing the pantry while I lay in bed trying, and failing, to sleep.

Hours later, the pain had not lifted, and I found myself staring at the bedroom window. It opens only about four inches, not even close to wide enough for a person to get through. But in that moment, it seemed like exactly the sort of idea despair likes to argue about. So, I texted her.

Me: "Tell me why you love me before I break the window latch, squeeze through the crack, and fall ten feet into a dog-shit-covered snowbank. Such is the level of my despair."

Gianna: "Babe stop that. I love you so much. You make us laugh and protect us and make sure we are happy and taken care of. And you love us for being ourselves."

Me: "You are only saying that because I threatened to break the window and drag snow and dog shit back into the house."

Gianna: "No I am not. Dog shit? I am dying over here."

I read her last line in the dark and laughed. Not the performed laugh. The real one. Gianna taught me something I had not known I needed: that humor could be a lifeline without being a lie.

I had always used laughter as armor, the quick joke that changed the subject, the self-deprecating aside that kept others comfortable and kept me hidden. That was the old kind of humor. Weaponized. Preemptive. It performed wellness to avoid the conversation about its absence.

What Gianna and I have developed is different. It is humor that tells the truth sideways, dark enough to name the despair, absurd enough to make it briefly bearable, and intimate enough that only someone who knew the whole story could receive it without alarm.

The exchange captures something the ten-point scale cannot. It shows what it looks like when two people build a shared language around an illness that does not announce itself politely. Gianna's response was not alarm, reassurance, or a careful clinical question. It was laughter that said: "I see you. I am not frightened. And I refuse to let this have the last word tonight."

That, too, is a form of medical assistance in living.

Gianna's, "I am dying over here," was exactly the right response. She knew what she was saying. She also knew what she was not saying.

That is the genius of a person who has learned to love Chief Dark Cloud.

I have lived with major depression since childhood. What follows is not a cure, a program, or a promise. It is simply how I try to stay alive and useful with an illness that, at its worst, tells me I should not exist.

Brains and bodies differ. What helps me may not help you. Some of the things I describe—hospitalization, being "formed" (involuntary detention), medications, ketamine—are serious medical interventions that must be handled by qualified professionals, not by memoirists or well-meaning friends.

If anything listed here is useful, take it as raw material, not instruction. If it isn't, leave it on the page.

The most practical tool I use is a simple 0–10 scale. It is not scientific. It is a way of forcing myself to look at my own condition with a bit more honesty, and to match my actions to the level of danger I am in.

When my number is low, my judgment is especially bad. I am most convinced that I am a burden and that others would be better off without me. The scale does not fix that, but it gives me a script to follow when my mind is lying.

If you recognize yourself in the lower numbers, please do not use that as confirmation that you are beyond help. Use it as evidence that you should talk to someone—a doctor, a therapist, a crisis service, or a trusted person who can help you get there.

Suicidal thinking is a health crisis, not a moral failure.

MY 0–10 SCALE

I don't rate how happy I am. I rate how safe I am inside my own mind. This is what the numbers mean for me.

0/10: Emergency

What it feels like:

- I have a specific plan to die, not just a wish to disappear.
- I feel certain that the world would be better off without me.
- I cannot imagine any future in which the pain changes.

What I do (or try to do):

- I treat this like chest pain, not like "having a bad day."
- This is my "hospital or psychiatrist now" level.

- If I can, I tell someone exactly what is happening: "I am at zero. I have a plan. I am not safe."

What others do:

- Stay physically with me if they can.
- Help me get to an emergency room, crisis unit, or urgent psychiatric care.
- If necessary, override my resistance and call for help anyway.

At zero, I cannot make good decisions about my own life. I have been issued an involuntary detention form for a seventy-two-hour hold in psychiatric ward twice. Each time I was deeply humiliated, but it kept me breathing long enough for the storm to pass.

1–3/10: The Sydney Carton Level ("It is a far, far better thing that I do...")

What it feels like:

- I am not actively taking steps to die, but I am rehearsing the speech: everyone would be freer, richer, lighter, if I were gone.
- I am withdrawing from people who love me because I feel like an infection.
- Ordinary tasks (shower, email, food) feel impossible or pointless.

What I do (or try to do):

- Tell someone I trust my number, even if I want to lie: "I'm at a three. Everything in me wants to say five, but it's three."

- Let others help with basic logistics: meals, appointments, childcare.
- Reduce my life to the smallest possible next steps: take meds if prescribed, drink water, sit in the same room as another human being, even silently.

What others do:

- They don't try to cheer me up with success, titles, or gratitude lists.
- They sit with me without demanding conversation.
- They remind me, gently, that I have been at three before and it did not stay three forever.
- If they think I am closer to zero than I admit, they push for medical help, even if I am angry with them.

At this level, I am vulnerable to any system that offers death as a tidy solution. This is my Sydney Carton level; self-erasure can look noble and rational from here. It is not.

4–6/10: Barely Functional to Just Managing

What it feels like:

- I can get through a day, but it feels like walking through waist-deep water.
- I can work, but my concentration is fragile, and my self-criticism is loud.
- I still think about death, but more as escape fantasy than active plan.

What I do (or try to do):

- Use work as a useful distraction, not as proof of my worth. When I can think about other people's problems, my own mind has less room to spiral.
- Keep some gentle structure: go to the office or a café, answer a few emails, show up for meetings even if I feel like an imposter.
- Avoid demanding too much from myself. This is not the level for grand new projects or major life decisions.

What helps:

- Reading in cafés, where I can be around people without having to be "on."
- Walking or easy hikes, including the trails around Uxbridge, Ontario.
- Talking to one safe person who understands that I am not asking them to fix it.

Hobbies—violin, chess, charcoal portraits—start to be possible at this level but often feel like accusations: "If you're really committed to getting better, you would enjoy this." I don't trust hobbies as treatment at four. I treat them as optional visitors.

7–8/10 : Better Days

What it feels like:

- The thought of death recedes. It might still be there, but in the background.
- I can feel small pockets of enjoyment without suspicion.
- I can believe, for hours at a time, that I am not a burden.

What I do (or try to do):

- Lean into the things that nourish me without needing to "earn" them: practicing violin badly, just for the sound, playing chess without turning it into a test of intelligence, drawing portraits that no one will ever see, hiking and noticing the light in the trees.
- Spend time in places that make me feel "substantial and intelligent," such as coffee with a colleague, an engrossing file, a mentoring conversation.

How I think about these days:

- This is when mentoring others helps my mood. Listening to someone else's story, especially with understanding and without judgment, reminds me that pain is survivable and that I have some use in this world.
- I try not to turn good days into pressure: "Now you must stay at eight forever."

They are evidence, not a contract.

9–10/10: Rare Air

I do not live at nine or ten. When I touch them, it is usually for a moment, a day when I am in love with my family and my work at the same time, when the air feels clear and the future open.

On those days:

- I remember that hope, not success or titles or grades or money, is the real medicine.
- I try to leave a few small things in place—a scheduled coffee, a trail I know I can walk, a person I know I can call —for the version of me who will soon be back at six, or four, or three.

I do not aim to live at ten. I aim to stay alive through zero.

Questions I Ask Myself When I'm Not Sure How I'm Doing

Depression is clever. It can make me say, "I'm fine," while I am quietly planning my death or say, "I'm in crisis," when I'm just exhausted. When I'm not sure where I am on the scale, I ask myself questions like these:

Have I thought about how I might die, or only that I am tired of living?
Vague thoughts of wanting to disappear are not the same as specific plans. Both matter. Plans mean danger.

Am I "tidying up" my life in ways that don't match my plans to live?
Giving things away, writing letters, making sure others will be "okay without me" can be rehearsals for leaving.

Have I stopped doing everything that usually helps, even a little?
When I abandon even the smallest anchors—coffee with a friend, short walks, basic hygiene—I know I am sliding.

Am I hiding from the people who know me best?
If I am dodging calls from the very people who would notice I'm unwell, that is usually data, not coincidence.

Can I imagine a future hour, day, or week that feels even slightly different from this one?
When the answer is honestly "no," I treat that as a symptom of the illness, not proof that the feeling is accurate.

These are not diagnostic criteria. They are ways of catching myself in my own lies.

If your answers to questions like these scare you, please do not treat that as a verdict on your worth. Treat it as a sign that you deserve help and attention, at least as much as you would if you were having chest pain or couldn't breathe.

Journaling and Tracking

I started journaling as a teenager. The early entries are mostly panic and self-loathing. For years, I only wrote when things were terrible. Even so, those pages became a kind of evidence against my own mind: proof that episodes did eventually ease, no matter how permanent they felt at the time.

That practice has evolved but never stopped. Journaling still helps me. Sometimes I simply write what I am feeling, in plain language. Other times, I track more systematically:

- my daily number on the 0–10 scale
- the medications I am taking and any changes in dose
- missed doses
- withdrawal symptoms or side effects when I am tapering off one drug or starting another
- life events that have rattled or upset me
- the quality and length of my sleep

Over weeks and months, patterns begin to show up. I can sometimes see that a drop in mood tracks closely with missed doses, or a medication change, or a run of short, broken nights. Other times I see that nothing "caused" the slide except the illness itself.

This kind of tracking does two things for me:

- It slows my thinking down. Instead of deciding, "This is all pointless," I must look at actual days, numbers, and notes.
- It prepares me for doctor's visits. When I walk into an appointment with concrete records—mood, meds, sleep,

events—I waste less time trying to remember and spend more time making decisions with my psychiatrist.

What it does not do is make me my own doctor. I do not change doses on my own based on my charts. The point of tracking is not to take over my treatment; it is to give better information to the people who are trained to treat me.

If you choose to track, it does not have to be elaborate. A notebook, a calendar, a notes app with a few quick lines per day is enough. The goal is not a perfect record. The goal is to give yourself and your clinicians a clearer, kinder view of what you are living through.

What My Family Does When I'm at 3 or Below

Depression isolates the person who has it and exhausts the people who love them. My family did not sign up to be a care team, but that is what they have sometimes become.

When I am at three or below on my scale, the things that help the most are small and unheroic:

- Gianna sits with me. Not to give speeches or strategies, but simply to occupy the same room. Presence is a form of oxygen.
- They lower the bar. They don't ask, "What's wrong?" when there is no clean answer. They ask, "Can I bring you some food?" or "Do you want me to make that call for you?"
- They help with logistics, refill prescriptions, drive me to appointments, manage childcare or household duties when I can't.

At low numbers, filling out a form or scheduling an appointment might as well be climbing a mountain. My family steps in to help.

- They also remember the past when I cannot.
- The remember the depression that feels permanent has always been cyclical, even when I insist otherwise. They remind me, gently, of other episodes that felt permanent but were not. They do not promise that I will "feel better tomorrow," but they point to concrete times when the fog eventually lifted.
- They take my safety seriously, even when I downplay it.

If I say I am at three, but they hear the language of zero, they do not accept my rating as gospel. They push for medical help, and they have been willing, when necessary, to involve professionals even when I found that humiliating.

None of this is easy for them. They are not saints. They are people who have been drafted into a war they did not choose. But their stubbornness has kept me alive more than once.

If you are the family member in this situation, it is not your job to cure someone else's depression. It is more like being a witness and a bridge: you help the person cross from isolation to care.

Treatments I've Tried

Because this is a memoir and not a medical textbook, I will keep this brief and general.

Over the years I have tried:

Medication.
Different antidepressants at different doses, under psychiatric care. Some helped, some did not, some helped for a time and then stopped. Side effects were sometimes significant. All this required trial, error, supervision, and patience.

Psychotherapy.
Talking with professionals who understood mood disorders and

trauma. At its best, therapy gave me language for what I was feeling and tools to notice the lies my mind tells when I am low.

Electroconvulsive therapy (ECT).
In my worst periods, ECT was part of my treatment. It is frightening, stigmatized, and imperfect. It is also one of the reasons I am still here.

Ketamine, prescribed off-label.
Ketamine, delivered in a medical setting, helped me for roughly two years. The acute lifting of suicidal thinking was real. It was not a permanent solution, but it bought me time and space.

Hospitalization and being formed (involuntary 72-hour hold).
I have been admitted voluntarily, and I have been formed against my will. There is no way to make that sound dignified. It is not. It is also, sometimes, the safest option when a person's judgment has been hijacked by illness.

Ordinary care.
Sleep. Food. Reduced alcohol. Time off work when needed. These are unfashionable compared to new treatments, but they matter.

I am describing these, not prescribing them. Each of these interventions carries risks, benefits, and trade-offs that must be weighed by a doctor and by the person living in the body that will bear them.

If you take anything from this section, let it be this: needing serious treatment for depression is not a moral failure. It is a sign that you are ill enough to deserve focused, competent care.

Sitting With Someone Else's Pain

One of the most useful things I have learned, both as a patient and as a lawyer and leader, is that you do not have to fix someone's pain to be helpful. You must be willing to stay near it.

In practice, that has meant the following:

At work, I give them time in private, listen without interrupting, and ask what they need rather than guessing. When a colleague is clearly struggling, I do not immediately reach for solutions or slogans. I try to listen rather than fix.

Sometimes the most powerful sentence a boss can say is, "You're not alone in this. Let's figure out what support looks like for you."

With friends and peers, I resist the urge to compare wounds or offer quick fixes. Instead, I might say, "I'm glad you told me, and "That sounds unbearable," and, "Can I stay with you a bit?"

With strangers, when I have spoken publicly about my own depression, people have entrusted me with their stories in foyers, hallways, and emails. My job in those moments is not to become their therapist. It is to acknowledge their courage, encourage them to seek proper help, and, when possible, point them toward resources.

Sometimes all a person needs in that moment is someone to sit next to them in their pain so they are not alone in it. You can be that person even if you do not know what to say. Especially if you do not know what to say.

Silence, accompanied by presence and respect, is often more healing than an armful of advice.

A Final Word

Depression has tried to convince me, repeatedly, that I am a problem to be solved or erased. The culture around me has sometimes cooperated in that lie, especially when it dresses death up as dignity.

What has kept me alive has not been success, titles, grades, or money. Those things have their place, but they do not cure despair. Hope does. And hope rarely arrives as a blinding revelation. It usually comes in smaller forms:

- a number on a scale honestly spoken
- a person who sits with you without flinching
- a nurse who closes a curtain gently
- a trail you know by heart
- a day when you feel, for an hour, "substantial and intelligent"

If this appendix helps anyone name their own number, ask for help, or sit a little longer with another person's pain, then the worst thing that ever happened to me will have been put to some use.

That is as close to a cure as I expect to find on this side of the ledger.

Acknowledgments

This book exists because people refused to let me disappear.

Adina Samuels saw this manuscript when it was raw and unwieldy and believed it was worth publishing. Her editorial instincts, patience, and willingness to take a chance on a story that does not fit neatly into any category gave this book its home at Entrechat Press. I am grateful for her trust and her craft.

Dr. Katy Kamkar read early drafts with the clinical precision and human warmth that define her work at CAMH. Her feedback sharpened the book's treatment of mental illness, and her willingness to champion it through her professional networks gave me confidence that the story might reach the people who need it most.

Nancy Dale, Gillian Burnett, Dr. Ramona Coehlo, and Christine Bazinet each read versions of this manuscript and offered the kind of honest, careful feedback that makes a writer braver. Their time and candor improved every chapter they touched.

Ian Kirby has been a mentor and friend across more years and more setbacks than either of us would have predicted. His faith in me—especially when I had given others good reason to withdraw theirs—helped me believe I could come back.

My earliest teachers shaped me before I had language for what they were doing. Mrs. Forrester and the late Mrs. Danos saw a boy from Weber Street and treated him as though he deserved their full attention. At St. Jerome's, the late Father Michael Cundari taught me to win with dignity and lose with pride—a lesson I have needed more often than I would like to admit.

To the psychiatrists, nurses, and staff who treated me during my hospitalization in 2009—I did not know all your names then, and I may never know them now. You did not try to fix me with slogans or congratulate me for surviving. You insisted, quietly and stubbornly, that my pain was not proof of my worthlessness. You provided what I have come to think of as medical assistance in living. That insistence saved my life.

To the colleagues and friends at the Ontario Bar Association, the Ministry of the Attorney General, and the Administrative Tribunals Support Service of Canada who supported my work and, in many cases, my recovery—thank you.

Adrienne, when I was polished and persuasive and wrong, you pleaded with the people who had the power to keep me alive. You would not let me talk my way out of living, and when that required fighting for me instead of with me, you fought. I did not understand what that cost you. I do now. That was the bravest kind of love.

Candace, Lizzie, and Emily—you have taught me everything I know about what is beautiful in life. Candace, you were my first reason to stay. Lizzie and Emily, you have grown up watching your father navigate an illness he cannot hide from you. Your stubbornness in loving me through the storms has taught me more about courage than any courtroom ever did.

Gianna, you married a man who came with weather warnings. You learned the shorthand of my ten-point scale, dragged me to Starbucks at three, slept in hospital chairs, and reminded me—sometimes bluntly, sometimes with a joke—that a depressed mind lies. You and the girls are the receipts.

To my father, Antonio Orlando Da Silva, and my mother, Delinah MacDonald—you carried your own wounds across oceans and decades, and you built what you could with what you had. This book is honest about the cost of that inheritance. It is also, I hope, evidence that something enduring came through.

To every person who approached me after a speech, sent a quiet email, or stopped me in a courthouse hallway to say that hearing my story made them seek help—you gave this book its purpose before it had a single page.

And to anyone reading this who recognizes themselves in the lower numbers: you are not beyond help. You are ill enough to deserve care. Please talk to someone.

This book is one inconvenient data point. I hope it is not the last.

A Note to the Reader Who Is Still in the Dark

I wrote this book for you.

Not the version of you sitting comfortably with a cup of coffee, reading someone else's story. I wrote it for the version of you at three in the morning, when the fog has settled and every thought your mind produces sounds like the truth.

I know that voice. It told me I was beyond help. It told me my suffering was permanent. It told me the people I loved would be better off without me. It told me these things with such authority that I believed them—not as opinions, but as facts.

If MAiD for mental illness had been available to me in my worst moments, I might have reached for it. Not because I truly wanted to die, but because my depressed mind was not a reliable narrator of my own worth, or of the permanence of my condition.

This book is the one I wish had existed when I was at my lowest—not to give me answers, but to give me time. To let me hear from someone who had been where I was and lived long enough to discover that the voice was wrong.

If you are in that place now, I am asking you to wait. Not because waiting is easy. Not because I can promise you the pain will vanish.

But because I have lived long enough to know that the mind that is telling you there is no way forward is the same mind that is sick. It may well be "competent" in every legal sense of that word while remaining unqualified, or unreliable, in making life-ending decisions on your own behalf.

Please reach out:

Talk Suicide Canada: 1-833-456-4566

Crisis Services Canada: 988

Kids Help Phone: 1-800-668-6868

If you want to bring "Opening Remarks" to your workplace, your profession, or your community—or if you simply want to tell me that this book reached you—I would be honoured to hear from you at ovdasilva@icloud.com.

And if this book helped you, consider passing it to someone who is still silent. Sometimes the most powerful thing you can do for another person is show them that someone survived.

www.ingramcontent.com/pod-product-compliance
Lightning Source LLC
LaVergne TN
LVHW100305210926
848480LV00003B/1028